NORMALIZATION OF DEVIANCE

THE THINGS THAT airlines, aircraft manufacturers, and the FAA are not sharing with the public. This book is the result of the author's doctoral research—*Safety Culture, Training, Understanding, Aviation Passion: The Impact on Manual Flight and Operational Performance.* While the intent of the research was to learn what predicted manual flight, what was learned may have predicted and, if heeded, prevented the Lion Air Flight 602, 2018 crash, Ethiopian Flight 302, 2019 crash, and Atlas Air Flight 3591, 2019 crash. What was learned could also have prevented the Air France Flight 447 crash. We now have the data that proves we can't simply blame the pilot.

There is never one reason an accident occurs, but a chain of events. If you travel, fly, or touch aviation in any aspect, you have every reason to read this book. If you wish to read the actual dissertation, it may be found at https://petittaviationresearch.com.

Inspiration. Motivation. Plane Stuff.

"Sometimes truth is scarier than fiction"

By Karlene K. Petitt

at

Flight To Success

www.KarlenePetitt.com

NORMALIZATION OF DEVIANCE

A THREAT TO AVIATION SAFETY

KARLENE K. PETITT, PhD

JET STAR PUBLISHING INC.
SEATAC WA

DEDICATION

I DEDICATE THIS work to the thousands of pilots worldwide who participated in this research, and to those who are courageous enough to use these results to create positive change.

Books by Karlene Petitt

Flight For Control
Flight For Safety
Flight For Survival
Flight For Sanity
Flight For Truth
Flight To Success, Be the Captain of Your Life
I Am Awesome, The ABCs of Being Me

TABLE OF CONTENTS

Author's Note 11

Synopsis 13

Introduction 17

Research Overview 25

1. Industry Concern 34

2. Automation Challenges 40

3. Beliefs and Perceptions 44

4. Trust and Complacency 50

5. Levels of Automation 53

6. Equipment Failure 55

7. Performance 59

8. Manual Flight 62

9. Pilot Error 67

10. Situation Awareness 69

11. Decision-Making 75

12. Experience 77

13. Confidence 84

14. Understanding...88

15. Training 98

16. Advanced Qualification Program (AQP)..............................104

17. Safety Culture and SMS...120

18. Aviation Passion...143

19. Literature Gap Review..149

20. Summary of Results...152

21. Recommendations...158

22. Conclusion..162

Appendix 1 Results...166

Definitions...180

Acronyms..186

References...188

Acknowledgements...207

About the Author 211

NORMALIZATION
OF
DEVIANCE

AUTHOR'S NOTE

NORMALIZATION OF DEVIANCE was a term that once identified pilots who didn't follow standard operating procedures and that behavior subsequently became the norm. Researchers identified that these employees didn't recognize their behavior as deviant because the behavior had subsequently become a normal occurrence within the organization. Today, this type of deviant behavior in the flight deck is rare due to standard operating procedures in automated aircraft. Rogue pilots are no longer able to perform in a manner conflicting with regulation, because modern day aircraft automatically report aircraft operations. However, normalization of deviance is not extinct. Research has identified that the current deviant behavior may have shifted from the flight line to corporate offices in the form of a negative safety culture.

Normalization of deviance is now the term that explains how an organization's culture and associated behavioral norms can violate FAA requirements and encourage pilots to perform in a manner contrary to written policy. It further explains how operators can know that pilots have insufficient knowledge, lack understanding, and are losing manual flight skills, yet they fail to improve training methodologies in order to increase the level of understanding. Furthermore, normalization of deviance may also explain how management can retaliate when employees follow the FAA mandate of *see something say something*. It's hard to imagine anyone retaliating against someone offering suggestions for safety, however, with a negative safety culture, manage by threat simply becomes a management style. A management style that has now been directly tied to operational performance.

Today, normalization of deviance is nothing more than an unacceptable term to justify illegal behavior in the corporate office. Illegal because federal law protects employees from retaliation for reporting safety concerns. Unacceptable because any adult who doesn't identify illegal behavior as wrong is fooling nobody. The problem arises when toxic leadership condones, supports, and perpetuates retaliatory behavior, and this becomes the norm within the organization. There is no question that such behavior is the core of a poor safety culture.

This book is the result of my doctoral research—*Safety Culture, Training, Understanding, Aviation Passion: The Impact on Manual Flight and Operational Performance*. Unless you are working toward a PhD, you would have no reason to read a dissertation. However, if you travel, fly, or touch aviation in any aspect, you have every reason to read this book. If you wish to read the actual dissertation, it may be found at https://petittaviationresearch.com.

This work would not be possible without the thousands of pilots who participated, others who reached out to locate pilots and encouraged them to respond to the study's survey, and all those who sent me comments, which I have included in this book. Our hope is that regulators and airlines heed the lessons learned, listen to the pilots' concerns, and take the appropriate action.

SYNOPSIS

THE OBJECTIVE OF my research was to understand pilots' preference for manual flight versus automation by identifying the relationships between 1) pilot training, 2) aircraft and systems understanding, 3) safety culture, 4) manual flight behavior, and 5) aviation passion. A survey instrument titled Manual Flight Inventory (MFI) was designed to gather and assess self-reported variables in these areas. Opinion-based questions were also asked to fully understand pilots' thoughts on automation, safety culture, policies, procedures, training methodologies and assessment measures, levels of understanding, and study techniques.

Exploratory Factor Analysis (EFA) was used to identify underlying factors from the data, followed by Confirmatory Factor Analysis (CFA) to test how well the measured variables represented the constructs. The measured variables were the results of the survey questions. The constructs were the factors— pilot training, aircraft and systems understanding, safety culture, manual flight behavior, and aviation passion. Structural Equation Modeling (SEM) was used to assess the causal relationships in order to either support or not support the hypotheses. For those who are interested the methodology and data collection process, please find the dissertation at https://petittaviationresearch.com. All references utilized in the original research can be found at the back of this book, as well as a list of definitions and acronyms. Superscript characters in the text indicate the reference work numbered at the end of the book.

In brief

The study began with the question as to why pilots were not manually flying their aircraft. Regulatory officials identified this to be a problem, not only with manual flight and skill loss, but lack of understanding of their equipment and associated displays. This was identified as a problem, and the Federal Aviation Administration (FAA) recommended all airlines to encourage manual flight.

While the intent of this research was to learn what predicted manual flight, what was learned may have predicted and, if heeded, prevented the Lion Air Flight 602, 2018 crash, Ethiopian Flight 302, 2019 crash, and Atlas Air Flight 3591, 2019 crash[275, 276, 277]. What was learned, if heeded, could also have prevented the Air France Flight 447 crash. There is never one reason an accident occurs, but a chain of events. At the core of all four of these accidents were failures in safety culture, reporting culture, pilot training, lack of understanding and, as a result, performance.

Most of the results were as expected, in that the significant predictors of manual flight were pilot understanding, pilot training, aviation passion, and safety culture. Whereas some might think that if a pilot didn't understand the aircraft and associated computer systems, they would be more inclined to manually fly—I believed that not to be the case.

Manual flight does not remove the necessity to understand the systems and utilize the information presented on the aircraft displays. Therefore, pushing buttons and allowing the aircraft to do its thing would be more comfortable for the pilot who lacks understanding. As it turned out, understanding of the aircraft operating systems had the greatest influence over a pilot's decision to manually fly.

The research identified the significant predictors of manual flight to be pilot understanding, pilot training, aviation passion, and safety culture. In the sequence of events from corporate processes to the flight line, the research identified that safety culture is the core of operational performance. Safety culture influences training, training influences pilots' level of understanding, and that level of understanding influences the pilot's decision to manually fly. Therefore, the answer as to why pilots are not flying their aircraft begins with safety culture.

Safety culture, as associated with Safety Management Systems (SMS), was also the greatest influencing factor over pilot training and operational performance. SMS and the significance to safety will be discussed later in this book. However, SMS is an FAA mandate to improve organizational performance and a positive safety culture is required as the foundation of any SMS. Pilot understanding is a direct result of pilot training, and current training practices are negatively influencing the decision for manual flight. As it turns out, the more a pilot trains in the airline environment, the less likely he or she is to manually fly their aircraft.

During my dissertation defense the question was posed, in response to the results, "*What do you think they will do?*" "They" referring to the FAA and the airline industry as a whole. We can only hope that industry executives and regulators alike will take note and will mandate improved training methodologies.

"*Sadly most pilots don't know how to fly anymore. When the weather or the traffic allowed, I often encourage my first officer to disconnect the automation and fly the approach, almost no one does it, in the last 5 years I think only 2 guys. People aren't comfortable. Is it because the Airbus doesn't feel right? Because the training we received, or the company policy, maybe a bit of all. One thing for sure, we got our wings clipped from the industry long time back and only those that do the extra mile to keep their skills risk sometime to be called in the office…*"

(Anonymous Pilot)

INTRODUCTION

"Automation is great: it makes us safer, and more aware, but I have so many thousands of hours on antiques, classic Lears, DC-9s, that I still appreciate old-school flying. The industry, as a whole, is losing important skills."

(Anonymous Pilot)

THE CONCERN FOR the level of understanding in relation to safety is highlighted throughout this book, and history has identified lack of understanding to be an ongoing problem. The question we must ask is whether technology itself is too complex or are pilots not being adequately trained. The answer appears evident in that as technology increases, airlines worldwide are being allowed to reduce training due to the higher levels of automation. This reduced training is contributing to accidents, incidents, and thousands of air safety reports. If training were to include improving the level of understanding of the advanced technology, I believe we would have less confusion and a far safer industry.

While automation was designed to improve safety, pilot training is not keeping up with technological growth, leaving pilots without a thorough understanding of aircraft systems and operational procedures that may result in pilots' reluctance to manually fly their aircraft without the autopilot and autothrust. The option to disengage the autothrust and autopilot remains in the pilot's control, but component failure may cause unintended disengagement requiring manual flight proficiency. Granted, highly automated aircraft have protective systems that will automatically correct pilot error such as overbanking and getting too slow while in manual flight. However, will pilots understand what to do if these automated features fail? Will they depend upon these automated features while in manual flight and not realize when the system is not working? Will they know what to do if they inadvertently select the wrong button? Pilots must be able to manage the aircraft in all modes of operation from Level 0 (no autopilot, autothrust, and flight director) to a fully automated and managed aircraft of Level 4 (autopilot, autothrust and flight director engaged). As you'll read later in this book, a senior captain at an international airline declared an emergency when he lost his autoflight system in VFR conditions, simply due to his discomfort of flying manually.

> *"If someone doesn't have manual flight routine… there is no situational awareness… with serious system failure onboard the a/c there will be no automation with a pilot with no manual flying routine there will be no situational awareness and a huge amount of stress!"*
>
> (Anonymous Pilot)

Pilots must be competent beyond rote memorization of aircraft limitations. They must understand the instrument displays, system operations, and operational procedures for full situation awareness (SA). SA is the ability to identify what's happening, understand the situation, and then be able to project that status into the future.[63] While research has identified that technology improves visualization in the glass cockpit aircraft, this technology could also be a contributing factor to reduced skills in the ability to scan. A glass cockpit refers to a flight deck with integrated electronic instrument displays versus analog digital flight instruments termed round-dial. The scan is an important aspect of flight where the pilot must be able to see, assess, and utilize the data for operational performance. There is concern that if the automation were to fail and pilots were required to fly on standby instruments, they may have problems maintaining control within the required speed, heading, and altitude control per the FAA required parameters.[273]

"I believe, that using automation correctly does help with situational awareness… especially in high density areas (think JFK or ORD [New York or Chicago]). But there are times when manual flight is safer, e.g. quickness of response, technical issues."

(Anonymous Pilot)

The Next Generation Air Transport System (NextGen) is underway, in which satellite-based systems will replace ground-based systems for air traffic management. This continued technological advancement will necessitate that pilots taxi using moving maps, execute satellite-based landing procedures, and assume responsibility for aircraft separation versus air traffic control (ATC) to manage that separation.[84] With increased complexity and additional responsibilities, reduced situational awareness will create an environment susceptible to human error.

Researchers have identified that significant changes in NextGen flight decks will not only provide new opportunities for error, but will also alter the nature and frequency of existing errors.[152] History has also shown that anytime new technology is introduced, a period of instability develops associated with a learning curve, creating an environment ripe for catastrophe.[218]

If pilots do not have a solid understanding of their aircraft and procedures, possessing both cognitive and physical skills, the added complexity of NextGen may increase instability with additional technological distractions. NextGen pilots will also have fewer opportunities to manually fly than they do today due to regulatory pilot-managed separation and automated arrivals. A paradigm shift is underway in which manual flight skills may become archaic due to NextGen, yet will remain essential for safe operations when systems fail. Thus, the necessity for pilots to understand and manage the automated aircraft, with or without the autopilot and autothrust engaged, remains a key issue in merging automated aircraft into the NextGen environment.

At the International Air Safety Summit conference in 2015, the Federal Aviation Administration's (FAA) chief scientific and technical advisor for the flight deck human factors group identified flight skill loss and mode awareness to be industry problems, but also included issues dealing with operational confusion (understanding), and guidance versus control.[2] In 2016 the Office of Inspector General (OIG) reported pilots' lack of hand flying skills and monitoring ability to be industry issues.[189] However, these industry concerns should be of no surprise, in that an FAA human factors task force reported similar issues in 1996, where pilots showed weaknesses in, "understanding, automation/mode awareness, and insufficient knowledge and skills."[71] The human factors task force also reported heightened concern with both "the quality and quantity of automation training."[71] Nineteen years after that 1996 report was presented to the human factors committee, the chair of that 1996 committee, spoke of those exact industry concerns at the 2015 IASS conference as if this were new information.

Unfortunately, recommendations from the 1996 FAA safety report went unaddressed, and planes have crashed and people have died due to inaction. Today flight skill loss due to automation reliance and complacency continues to grow as an industry concern.

Unheeded concerns contained within that 1996 FAA report were contributing factors to numerous accidents, incidents, and thousands of events resulting from pilot error.[71] An accident is identified when any person suffers death or serious injury on an aircraft or in which the aircraft receives substantial damage. An incident could be any number of events that could fail with potential to affect the safety of the operation or damage to the aircraft. The primary difference between the two is the level of damage and whether someone dies.

A 2013 FAA sponsored working group (WG) examined 46 major incidents and accidents, 734 Aviation Safety Reporting System (ASRS) reports, 9155 Line Operations Safety Audits (LOSA), and interviewed numerous pilots.[79] This working group identified insufficient understanding of aircraft systems, overuse of automation, and flight skill loss, associated with training, to be contributing factors to pilot error. In response to the concern for flight skill loss, the FAA released a 2013 safety alert requesting operators to encourage manual flight.[76] Despite this FAA directive it appears that pilots are still reluctant to manually fly their aircraft; therefore, flight skill loss has become an industry issue.

The problem with the reluctance to manually fly is that it diminishes pilots' skills which may be a result of and/or contributing factor to the lack of confidence. Lack of confidence will then perpetuate the reluctance.

The nature of long-haul flying has also created additional challenges in the area of pilot competency and performance. Reduced vertical separation minimums (RVSM) require autopilot usage enroute to enable aircraft to maintain them. Technology also enables aircraft to stay aloft for many hours which carries with it the many challenges for maintaining currency, and of great concern is how that currency is managed with a check the box mentality.

Many FAA approved training programs require pilots to train themselves at home. The classroom portion of training then becomes a review of what will be asked on the electronic test. The electronic test has become the assessment measure of pilots' knowledge versus a traditional oral exam. Unfortunately, the electronic test is incapable of assessing the level of understanding as that oral once had. There is no way to know whether or not the pilot understands the systems without speaking to the pilot. The simulator portion of training often allows the pilot to only experience an event once, despite that in order to learn pilots must have the ability to practice.

General aviation flight activity also impacts a pilot's decision to disengage automation during a revenue flight. The pilots' passion may also transfer to the job with greater interest resulting in self-directed learning. Thus, the question of whether passion could overcome all other obstacles was the reason passion became part of the research. Safety culture, policy, and training methodologies also impose additional factors that impact pilot behavior concerning manual flight.

Within the advanced qualification program (AQP)—a train to proficiency program introduced in 1990—pilot training has shifted from individual performance assessment to crew-based performance assessment.[120] Under AQP guidelines, airlines have realized an economic benefit by reducing the training footprint—less training. However, training assessment effectiveness has been an ongoing concern and may still be in question, in that pilots are passing training, but thousands of safety reports are being filed monthly. Therefore, reduced training should be questioned, as well as *how* that training is being conducted.

This raises the question as to how AQP training has impacted pilots' aircraft systems and operational understanding, confidence, monitoring skills, and willingness to manually fly. The first step in finding a solution to these industry problems—flight skill loss, lack of mode awareness and confusion, lack of manual flying and monitoring skills, and lack of aircraft understanding and overuse of automation—was to understand how current training practices, pilots' understanding, safety culture, and passion, impact performance and pilots' reluctance to manually fly.

NextGen will increase pilot responsibility, adding more complexity and creating opportunities for error. Therefore, the 2018 safety management systems (SMS) was designed for operators to evaluate the environment, assess hazards, mitigate risk, and capture errors.[77] In the middle of these two spectrums of safety, NextGen and SMS, pilot performance becomes an integral part of the entire system. However, SMS requires a positive safety culture. Not only is SMS nonexistent with a negative safety culture, safety culture also impacts pilot training, and training is negatively impacting operational performance. How can training negatively impact performance? Those answers will follow.

Study Significance

THE RESEARCH IDENTIFIED that safety culture significantly influences pilot training and, hence, operational performance. The results also identified that current training practices are negatively influencing the decision for manual flight. Pilots' understanding of their aircraft also impacts the decision to manually fly, and understanding is a direct result of training. Training is a direct result of safety culture.

Current industry reports have identified performance issues in modern 'glass cockpit' aircraft have resulted in accidents, incidents, and thousands of safety reports. Whereas current literature has identified automation challenges—including trust and reliability, complacency, display and integrated systems design, confidence, and situation awareness—there was a gap in the research as to what factors impacted pilots' performance and proclivity toward automation usage, and whether automation usage impacted performance. In addition, while much research has been conducted on safety culture, another gap in the research existed as to how safety culture impacted pilot training, and aircraft understanding and therefore a pilot's willingness to manually fly. These gaps have now been filled with this research. The problems do not lay in the hands of the pilots, but in the negative safety culture of airlines worldwide, where training does not ensure an adequate level of understanding and is ultimately causing pilot error. The question is—*what will they do?*

Research Overview

THE OVERARCHING RESEARCH questions were: "Does pilot training, aircraft understanding, aviation passion, and safety culture, impact a pilot's decision as to the level of automation usage? To what extent do these factors impact each other? Could demographics such as age, gender, geographic location, flight hours, type of aircraft, or general aviation flight, impact pilots' performance associated with the level of automation utilized?"

Aviator performance regarding manual flight has become an industry problem, but factors impacting this performance had yet to be determined, until now. In the research, the level of performance identified how the aviator chose to operate the aircraft indicated by the level of automation selected, not how well they flew. Yet, the FAA clearly recognizes the relationship between manual flight and pilot proficiency because they recommended that pilots should manually fly their aircraft.[76] Yet, despite that recommendation, the OIG reported pilots continue to lack hand-flying skills and lack monitoring ability.[189] Pilots' unwillingness to manually fly has been identified as an industry problem, but the specific reasons for this unwillingness had yet to be identified or acknowledged. Therefore, my doctoral research was designed to better understand this problem.

To begin the process, a survey instrument—Manual Flight Inventory (MFI)—was developed, tested, and validated to conduct this research. MFI was designed to assess self-reported variables with a measurement tool not previously validated or used, thus considered new scale development.

The briefest explanation of exploratory factor analysis (EFA), confirmatory factor analysis (CFA), and structural equation modeling (SEM) is that these are all statistical analysis programs. The programs were utilized to analyze the data collected on the survey instrument.

In that this research was based upon new scale development, exploratory factor analysis (EFA) was used to extract underlying factors among selected input variables in the analysis. After EFA was run, hypotheses were formed. A confirmatory factor analysis (CFA) measurement model was then built and tested. Structural equation modeling (SEM) was used to test the relationships between factors in order to better understand the underlying correlations that could influence pilot behavior where manual flight and a variety of variables were concerned. The MFI survey was developed to better understand these relationships in order to assist the aviation industry in better equipping itself to comprehend and solve the problem. Details on the process with further explanation on methodology can be found in the dissertation at https://petittaviationresearch.com.

Delimitations

DELIMITATIONS ARE THE characteristics defining the boundaries of the study. Meaning, what guidelines did I create and the rationale for doing so. The following information is the *how* and the *why* of the parameters I chose.

Multiple factors could impact a pilot's willingness to manually fly, but it would be impossible in one research project to asses all the possibilities. Thus, this research focused only on pilot training, pilots' systems understanding, safety culture, aviation passion, and the level of automation usage. Fatigue was not included in this research, but does impact manual flight and performance. That study is coming.

The population studied included airline, charter, and corporate/fractional pilots, worldwide, in multiple aircraft types. Pilot instructors and check airman were allowed to participate, even though these training professionals should have higher levels of understanding than average line pilots. Pilots employed in single pilot operations were not invited to participate because single pilot operation may necessitate higher automation use to reduce workload to a manageable level. Many active pilots sit reserve and may not fly during the year, and many receive recurrent training on an annual basis. Therefore, pilots who have retired or were between jobs within the previous twelve calendar months, were allowed to participate. The pilots who were retired, or between jobs within a year, were perceived to still have enough recent experience and perception of past behavior to be of value. Pilots who were in the middle of training with a new company, or on a new aircraft type, were requested to respond with answers based upon the most recent aircraft in which they had experience.

To ensure pilot opinions were based on their experience and not a perception of what they thought could be the case, the questions were designed to be non-conditional. For example, a domestic pilot was not requested to state their opinion on using automation at the end of a long-haul flight they never experienced. Each automation opinion-based question was designed to allow the pilot to answer based upon their experience and frame of reference.

The research was not intended to study pilots within an individual country or employed by a specific operator, but was designed to be a broad view of the worldwide pilot population, therefore demographic data was collected based upon general geographic locations.

Limitations and Assumptions

LIMITATIONS ARE A part of life, and the heart of any research. Due to the scope of the research, and the fact that it involved humans that spanned the globe, there were limitations within the research. As a researcher, we are required to identify those limitations, but also provide assumptions as to why we did what we did. Following are both my limitations and assumptions within the original research.

A potential limitation of this study was the lack of a perfect sampling frame due to expansive worldwide operations, which necessitated relying on nonprobability sampling. A sampling frame would be a master list of all worldwide pilots that I could randomly sample. Therefore, the sample (pilot participants) was primarily located through social network systems (SNS). SNS are virtual platforms where pilots connect and communicate. I utilized a hybrid of snowball sampling, respondent drive sampling, and purposive sampling.

This sample could also be biased toward pilots with a higher passion for aviation, who would be more apt to be motivated for self-directed learning than a pilot whose only interest was the perception of a large paycheck. However, many pilots also connect to these sites for the sole purpose of shifting jobs and searching for better career opportunities, thus participation could be career-motivated versus passion driven.

Posting a survey link on the open Internet also had the risk of anyone who had access, to potentially taking it. In order to locate and target my population, and avoid just anyone from taking the survey, I created a labyrinth of processes to make it more difficult to find. More than that, I provided no incentives to further discourage anyone outside the pilot demographic from taking it only to win a prize. Precautions were taken to never post the survey link to any SNS public forum, but to direct potential participants to visit my blog that would present qualifications and request participation. From my blog, potential participants were then directed to a website that reiterated required qualifications, and further explained the purpose, history, and declaration of anonymity before the participant accessed the survey link.

As the researcher, I was part of the target population. I am also an author with a public domain and active on SNS, therefore a potential limitation could have been the inability to separate my scholarly work from that of personal opinions, aviation activity, publications, and blogging activity. However, there is no indication in the research or otherwise that this was the case. Regardless, precautions were taken to design the survey questions so my public profile would not influence how the participants responded. To separate the industry-related issues and opinions from the survey, a survey link was never connected to an aviation industry statement, and the link to the survey was only posted on the Petitt Aviation Research site. The research site included history, purpose, and qualifications to participate specific to the research.

There was a question as to whether or not I could influence another pilot in how they answered the survey, by using social media to ask them to take it. While this was statistically proven to be inaccurate, I found the challenge interesting. *Could a pilot who was part of the demographic have the power to control the response of other pilots by simply by asking them to perform a task?* This led to personality research and revealed some interesting facts. Pilot personality profiles revealed that pilots are emotionally stable extroverts who are highly conscientious and hold strong opinions. The data indicate that a greater percentage of pilots may not to be open or agreeable to new ideas. Therefore, the assumption was made that pilots would not be swayed by opinions of another, but were more than willing to stand up to their belief system.

Research further identified political opinions on Twitter, noted as opinion leadership, regarding influence of political participation, and found that Twitter use indicated a person's involvement in the political processes but did not necessarily support a person's engagement. Meaning, Twitter did not fully sway these individuals, albeit they may have been involved in viewing and responding to statements.

Both online and paper surveys were initially utilized to avoid potential limitations of one methodology versus the other. However, research has identified there is no discernable difference between data collection formats with online versus paper surveys.[208] Thus, there was no reason to expect that the pilot population would have different results between paper and online surveys. The primary assumption was that the pilots would tell the truth when taking the survey. There was also the assumption that those taking the online survey were in fact who they claimed to be, and therefore part of the target population.

As with any survey, self-reported data could be subject to accuracy bias, meaning the measurement is true. The surveyed pilots may have an inflated self-perception versus actual knowledge. Research indicates that people may also remember successes more than failures, thus inaccurately overestimate their own abilities. In a 1991 study of judges and college professors, it was identified that there was no difference in overestimation in that 94% of college professors surveyed believed they were better than their colleagues;

and 90% of federal judges considered themselves above average as compared to their peers.[41] Therefore, the pilot may indicate a higher level of knowledge, ability, or performance than he or she actually has. However, reporting higher than actual ability could be equally, or more, prevalent during a live interview due to the respondent feeling uncomfortable in reporting low knowledge and performance to the interviewer versus an on-line or paper survey.

A number of precautions were taken to eliminate accuracy bias, including emphasis upon anonymity, clearly defined goals, and survey question structure. Pilots' names, and the name of their employer, were not asked; therefore, performance was not linked to the pilot or company. A detailed explanation as to the purpose of this research was provided to promote participation. Survey questions were designed in a manner to assist the pilot respondent in answering the question, without forcing the pilot to select one extreme or another. Then tests were conducted to assure validity and reliability of the survey instrument.

Despite the precautions to encourage participants to respond honestly, the limitation of assessing the level of pilot understanding, without an actual test to determine knowledge, could be reflective of pilots' overconfidence in their knowledge more than their actual understanding. *Confidence* was removed as a factor due to potential high cross-loading with the factor labeled *Understanding*. However, the factor Understanding could also reflect confidence versus actual knowledge. Meaning—did the pilot know the answer, or were they simply highly confident that they might know.

The greatest overall limitations were potentially (a) demographics of a worldwide sample associated with misunderstood questions due to language barriers, (b) company and manufacturer mandates dictating automation usage, and (c) the vast number of potential situations that would impact a pilot's decision to manually fly. First, while English is the required language of pilots worldwide, there was potential for a conceptual misunderstanding of the questions when English was the second language for many participants. Second, many companies and aircraft manufacturers have a variety of automation mandates, beyond government regulations, that could leave the pilot without a choice for manual flight. In addition to written policies, results identified unwritten policies were a factor. Third, the combination of potential reasons a pilot chooses automation over manual flight are far too many to capture in one survey instrument. The increased length of adding those types of questions would have greatly increased the risk of survey fatigue where the pilot would quit prior to completion. Moreover, by eliminating questions that might not pertain to everyone, pilots could answer based upon their actual experience.

Finally, there was a limitation for the pilots who were currently operating in today's environment but had not received initial training under the current system. This group of pilots' responses would most likely impact the questions regarding an oral assessment versus an electronic test, and who were trained in a non-AQP environment. However, this limitation would have softened the results.

"I want to point out one thing that stood out to me in the survey. There were several questions that asked about my initial training on my aircraft. The answers I provided would be different if I were doing that training today. I initially trained on my aircraft 20 years ago and upgraded to Captain on it 11 years ago. The training today is very different than it was back then."

(Anonymous Pilot)

There were also expatriate pilots that were not identified as a category, and should have been. These are pilots who identify and trained with one culture but fly in another. For example, a European pilot who is now flying on contract in Asia. Also, some of these pilots may have been trained at one company and yet fly for another.

> *"A few of my responses may have been skewed by the fact that questions regarding initial training on my current aircraft (B747-400/-8) did not occur at my current company (my 3rd airline on the same aircraft type), but I came up with the best answers I could for your research."*
>
> *(Anonymous Pilot)*

While there are limitations with any study and everything contains bias, the assumption was that this research would take the industry one step closer to answering the questions that could support operational safety in the airline industry.

1. Industry Concern

"Automation can be an improvement to safety. But at the end of the day, we still need pilots with a high level of flying skills and the ability to recognize when automation is being helpful, and when it becomes a distraction and a threat. Unfortunately, today's training environment is too centered (in my opinion) on automation and discourages us from thinking like aviators."

(Anonymous Pilot)

HUMAN ERROR IS not a new event. As long as humans continue to build and operate aircraft, human error will be an integral component of research, design, development, and training. The history of aviation safety has evolved from an equipment focus, to integrating human factors, and is progressing into the organization as a whole with aviation Safety Management Systems (SMS). Much has been learned by analyzing accidents and pilot safety reports, which have driven safety efforts. Yet, despite known concerns, history repeats with aircraft accidents, incidents, and safety reports attributed to automation dependency, confusion, limited knowledge, communication errors, mode awareness, flight skills, and inadequate training.[79] When automated glass flight deck aircraft entered the industry, a 1996 FAA human factors safety report identified pilots' weaknesses in aircraft understanding and automation mode awareness due to inadequate knowledge and skill, and further expressed concern for weak automation training with both quality and quantity of training.[71] Two decades later, similar performance issues prevail despite advanced automation and AQP training methodologies.

The industry has attempted to address performance issues. As the result of the Colgan Air Flight 3407 crash during arrival into the Buffalo-Niagara International Airport (12 Feb 2009), the Airline Safety and Pilot Improvement Act of 2009 was introduced into Congress, yet never passed the Senate.[37] The act, however, introduced regulatory change to increase flight hours for the airline transport pilot (ATP) certificate to 1500 hours, which was subsequently adopted into regulation in 2010.[78] While an FAA representative told me that the 1500-hour change had been underway long before the Colgan Air 2009 accident, this flight hour change was attributed to be the result of that accident, despite neither of the pilots having less than 1500 hours. The captain had a history of proficiency issues.

Nevertheless, where experience was once valued and identified by the number of flight hours a pilot acquired, the quality of experience associated with performance under automation brings into question the value of automated aircraft flight hours.[115] As an example of flight hours not supporting performance enhanced experience, the pilots in a series of catastrophic airline crashes— Colgan Air Flight 3407 (2009), Air France Flight 447 (2009), Asiana Flight 214 (2013), and UPS Flight 1354 (2013)—were anything but novice, as these pilots' combined experience exceeded 50,000 flight hours. While these accidents were attributed to pilot error due to inadequate skill, critical analysis revealed problems beyond skill to include lack of systems and aircraft understanding, and incorrect operational procedures.

Legislation followed the Airline Safety Act of 2009, resulting in the Airline Safety and Federal Aviation Extension Act of 2010.[108] Regulatory implementation of National Transportation Safety Board (NTSB) recommendations toward pilot performance, to include stall training, upset recovery training, remedial training programs for performance deficiencies, stick pusher training, and weather training, became public law in 2010. An FAA 2019 simulator mandate now requires training to include manually flown arrivals and departures, slow flight, loss of reliable airspeed, and recovery from bounced landings.[189] Current legislation and regulatory mandates have focused on flight training—pertaining to simulator training—yet did not address knowledge training, or assessment measures to ensure understanding.

Despite this legislation, a preponderance of research has identified pilot confusion and lack of understanding to be causal factors of inadequate performance, resulting in accidents, incidents, or pilot safety reports. The Air France Flight 447 crash is a poignant example of hull loss attributed to pilots' inability to fly their aircraft with degraded levels of automation, yet the pilots' lack of understanding of the Airbus A330 operating systems may have attributed to the crash.[19] Air Transat Flight 236 presents yet another accident where pilot confusion created a total fuel loss condition, with a subsequent dual engine failure in an Airbus A330.[54] While lack of systems understanding caused this event, the captain's manual flight skills enabled him to safely land a powerless jet. This old school pilot with glider experience presents a poignant example as to why manual flight ability is an essential skill. Even when the worst happens, if the pilot can fly there is hope of survival.

Flight skill loss due to pilot dependence upon automation presents an additional concern. Current flight training requirements do not provide guidance, do not mandate manual flight performance, do not require practice in the simulator, and do not require the pilot to demonstrate manual flight performance in the aircraft with a training professional. However, as reported at the 2015 IASS conference, the FAA has considered a mandate for pilots to be required to manually fly with passengers, despite never having demonstrated proficiency in the aircraft. As you will learn, the question as to what constitutes 'manual flight' is still open for discussion.

In response to the flight skill loss concern, the FAA released a 2013 safety alert that encouraged pilots to disengage the autopilot and autothrottle, to manually fly the aircraft in order to maintain manual flying skills. However, flight skills extend beyond manual flight to operational performance of aircraft management, incorporating both knowledge and procedural performance. A 2013 FAA working group (WG) further reported operational performance concerns due to insufficient aircraft systems knowledge, procedures, and understanding the aircraft condition.[79] Therefore, pilots may have difficulty when failures occur and there are no written procedures or guidance, resulting in the flight crews' inability to respond properly

The Lion Air, Flight 610 (MAX) crash of 2018, Ethiopian Flight 302, (MAX) crash of 2019, and Atlas Flight 3591, crash in 2019, are all poignant examples of the findings of the working group and this research. The inability for a pilot to identify a faulty system and understand how to deactivate it when the system faulted is a question of understanding, and one attributed to training. Regardless of an automated system failing and driving the nose down, at a critical phase of flight, pilots should be able to identify the failure and to stop a nose down motion—despite the reason why. But nothing is as simple as it appears. Prior to the Ethiopian crash the pilots received an erroneous stall warning due to a faulty system, immediately after takeoff. Movement of flaps then activated the MCAS system. A system that the pilots had no idea existed. These pilots had never been trained. The day prior to the Lion Air crash, the activation of this MCAS system erroneously activated stabilizer movement and the pilots responded correctly but cutting out the stabilizer trim switches. Maintenance received this information, yet they took no action and the plane continued in service.

What's most disturbing about these accidents is that negative safety culture was a primary factor, where economics were placed before training by the manufacturer and airlines alike. Lack of information sharing was a key failure in the safety culture of both airlines and the manufacturer. The Atlas accident further identified the pilots' inability to understand what the aircraft was doing and how to manage it during an unintended mode change. The crew inadvertently activated the go-around mode and failed to disengage the autopilot in order to recover. They fought the airplane all the way to impact. Either they lacked understanding how to reconfigure, or they lacked mode awareness.

While Airbus reported that 70-90% of aviation accidents have been attributed to pilot error, pilot error is not an isolated causal factor.[7] An accident is rarely due to one event, but a chain of events that necessitates a system analysis.

> "If the problem can be judged to lie exclusively in the head and heart of an unworthy flight crew, then no one in the system needs to be responsible for changes and improvements. False comfort is gained when the irresponsible pilot is the only threat."
>
> Robert Besco

Technology has shifted to enable aircraft to remain airborne for extended periods of time. This requires multiple pilots due to crew duty limitations, yet only one pilot will receive the experience of a takeoff and landing per flight segment. Reduced Vertical Separation Minimums (RVSM), is airspace between FL290 and FL 410 (29,000 and 41,000 feet) in which automated aircraft are able to pass within 1000 feet.[81] However, RVSM airspace further limits the opportunity for a pilot to manually fly the aircraft because autopilot usage is mandated. Regulations and company requirements also exist for automation usage during low visibility approaches.

Unfortunately, pilots' lack of opportunity to manually fly the aircraft will continue to increase due to NextGen operations, further reducing manual flight opportunities. The concern for pilot error in automatic aircraft versus analog aircraft was expressed when the researchers identified that human errors made in a modern aircraft were more likely to end in an accident due to an input-output effect that becomes a compounded chain of events.[178] The Air France Flight 447, crash is an example of a compounded chain of events. Therefore, understanding automation challenges of complex highly automated aircraft becomes essential. **Note:** For a detailed explanation of AF447, I recommend the book: *Understanding Air France 447* by Captain Bill Palmer.[192]

> *"Companies are more focused on their short-term statistics and strongly discourage disconnecting the automation. This has a negative impact on our handling and safety as we get less and less practice. Hopefully the future results of your survey will be significant and you'll be able to show them to the authorities."*
>
> (Anonymous Pilot)

2. Automation Challenges

"Automation can be an improvement to safety. But at the end of the day, we still need pilots with a high level of flying skills and the ability to recognize when automation is being helpful, and when it becomes a distraction and a threat."

(Anonymous Pilot)

WITH THE ADVENT of glass cockpit and fly-by-wire technology, airliner operation has shifted from flying with skill to managing systems with knowledge application. Automated aircraft represent the core of aircraft operations today, and knowledge application requires understanding aircraft systems, more so than learning what buttons to push.

Human factors and aircraft design are integrated to achieve efficient information-processing displays in order to improve safety. Automation interface is not only an autoflight system display, but flight control functionality. Disengaging the autopilot, flight director, and autothrust does not necessarily remove computer control in a fly-by-wire aircraft, yet disengagement is considered manual flight. When a pilot manually operates a fly-by-wire aircraft, depending upon the level of computer failures or level of automation selected, computers assist behind the scenes controlling surface movements to provide more efficiency. This functionality removes the pilot from traditional flight control management thought processes. Pilots once flew an aircraft with a yoke in a cockpit, connected to a cable that directly controlled flight control surfaces. Today a pilot manages a fly-by-wire aircraft with a control stick or yoke that sends a command from a flight deck through wires to computer actuators that move control surfaces to achieve computer-desired performance, per the pilot's command. Errors in numerous accidents have been, in part, due to system designers' inability to identify and acknowledge the impact of pilots' interaction with automation, the pilots' expertise, and the type of automated systems training afforded them.[241]

"Flying fully automated aircraft with no previous years of experience and lots of manual flying can be a big threat."

(Anonymous Pilot)

———————

Early fly-by-wire aircraft were designed to be harmonized in order to meet certification requirements. Continuing developments demand fly-by-wire technology to reduce weight, as well as the reduction of maneuver capabilities to prevent control loss, which in turn prohibits additional control actions. While improving passenger comfort, this technology has resulted in increased complexity of flight control computers. This added complexity, however, creates more confusion for operating crews.

Confusion extends beyond operations to what constitutes manual flight, as there is a taxonomy difference between the OIG and the FAA. Line operation safety audit (LOSA) defines manual flight as related to vertical, lateral, or speed deviations, and power settings, indicating both autothrust and autopilot are disengaged, yet the flight director is not mentioned.[79] The OIG identified manual flight as only the autopilot disengaged, with the autothrust and flight directors engaged. This concern is most alarming because the OIG identified manual flight to be a problem, meaning that even with the autothrust engaged pilots are having problems flying their aircraft.

Full manual flight indicates no automation—autoflight, autothrust or flight directors.[189] *Full autoflight* indicates that the autopilot, autothrust, and flight director are engaged, and the aircraft is being flown per pilot programmed commands without mode control panel interventions—the concept of a NextGen operation.[84] To add to the confusion, tactical autoflight indicates that the autopilot, autothrust, and flight director are engaged, but the aircraft pilot manages heading, speed, and altitude interventions.[189] Current operations dictate both types of automation usage—full autoflight and tactical. Aircraft are programed for full autoflight with a departure, route and arrival, yet tactical autoflight is used during Air Traffic Control (ATC) interventions. The question remains—if the FAA requests pilots to manually fly their aircraft, do the pilots know what manual flight means? It turns out they are equally confused as the industry leaders.

> *"The Boeing 777 autothrottle remains connected all the time. We are encouraged and do fly "manually" below 10000 feet, with the autopilot off. Some questions may give the impression that we do not do any "manual" flying because we always have the autothrottle connected."*
>
> (Anonymous Pilot)

"Important topic. We put a lot of emphasis on manual flight. Autopilot off means autothrust off in my company. Manual flying is generally allowed, and in high regard, depending on the situation."

(Anonymous Pilot)

The focus of automation research, however, has revolved around digital displays in a glass cockpit and integrated system designs—versus the traditional round-dial aircraft. Limited discussion exists on flight control operations and understanding of the added complexity of the fly-by-wire system. When integrated displays are lost the crew may be left with minimal operational understanding.

The Air France Flight 447 crash indicates that aircraft management may not depend solely upon mode awareness, but on a deeper understanding as to what the displayed information (or absence of it) indicates and how to manage the systems to achieve flight management goals. Beyond understanding aircraft displays, automation challenges include pilot perceptions, trust, and complacency, as well as technology related to the levels of automation and equipment failure.

3. Beliefs and Perceptions

*"I hear and read that many Companies in the World
require and mandate full automation during the whole
flight...what I think of it is that it is counterproductive to
safety! I agree that the autopilot flies better than a human,
but it flies only what the human tells it to fly!"*

(Anonymous Pilot)

HUMAN FACTORS AND automation research has shifted over the years. Early automation research (1990s) focused on behaviors and attitudes toward automation usage and reliance. Pilots historically felt more comfortable manually flying than using the automation. Performance was not necessarily connected to the individual's expectations or automation reliability, but pilots were initially reluctant to fully utilize automation and defaulted to manual flight.[194] This reluctance was observed to be due to a lack of knowledge of the computer system. I was instructing on the B757 during this time and witnessed pilots disengage the automation to take control because they did not understand the flight management system (FMS). These early pilots also had exceptional manual flight skills to fall back on. As their knowledge, comfort, and skill with the automation grew, they were more willing to use the automation. Success in accomplishing a task is said to be, in part, dependent upon the perception of that success.[41] As pilots' confidence increased (or perception of that ability) automation use increased, and ultimately resulted in automation dependence.

A challenge for researchers became the difficulty in readily understanding why pilots were reluctant to disengage their automation and manually fly their aircraft by simply asking them. In the search for automation perceptions, researchers identified pilots' lack of understanding, poor attention, limited knowledge, mode awareness issues, and problems managing an automation surprise resulted from automation complexity.[95]

However, researchers later assessed pilot perceptions of automation and identified five automation issues, including:

- ✈ lack of understanding
- ✈ automation function may not be transparent
- ✈ pilot overconfidence in the automation
- ✈ poorly designed equipment
- ✈ inadequate training[176]

While early research claimed aircraft complexity to be a cause of automation problems, current researchers, more accurately so, believe that complexity is not necessarily the issue, but inadequate training on the complex aircraft to be the problem.[95, 178]

"The problem arises when folks don't understand the auto-mation & what level of automation to use at which stage of flight. Boeings have been far more conventional in their approach to ergonomics & the 'Man-Machine' interface... where the bond is a lot stronger! I feel that I'm still a rookie in this aircraft, having flown the Baby 'Bus [A320] for a little over 10 years, as it still foxes me into saying, 'Oh shit! What now???'"

(Anonymous Pilot)

———————

Pilot beliefs and perceptions were also identified in pilot comments. It was difficult to determine where to place the following comments within this book because they identified either a lack of systems understanding, misperceptions of what another company is doing, or assumptions on manufacturer mandates that may not be fact. These comments could also be reflective of company policy, training practices, or historic experiences that no longer apply.

"Airbus aircraft can't land with auto-thrust on. At 20 feet (manual landing), the aircraft will order "Retard! Retard!" so the pilot will close the thrust levers, thereby disengaging the auto-thrust."

(Anonymous Pilot)

———————

The Airbus has non-moving thrust levers and will automatically provide thrust for the active mode between an idle thrust lever position and the climb (CL) detent. In a fully automated approach (LAND mode) the thrust automatically goes into a Retard mode and remains there until after landing. At 10 feet the plane calls out "Retard! Retard!" to remind the pilot to bring the thrust levers to idle to match (confirm) the automatic idle power setting, enabling the pilot to select reverse thrust. In a landing with the autopilot disengaged the 20 foot "Retard! Retard!" is telling the pilot to reduce thrust for landing. However, the autothrust does not disconnect until it reaches the idle detent. The only way to fully assess if a pilot were to have this understanding, would be from an oral exam.

> *"Flying Airbus, rarely did we disconnect A/T during an approach, whereas Boeing encourages manual flight. So, I would have answered very differently had I still been flying Airbus."*
>
> *(Anonymous Pilot)*

> *"Just to add some extra information it might be worth noting that like you I fly the B777 and our company and I believe BOEING mandates the use of the autothrottle at all times."*
>
> *(Anonymous Pilot)*

The above two statements conflict with each other, but neither of these pilots are wrong. They are simply expressing a belief of what was told to them by their respective airlines, representative culture.

> *"The US and EU methods of training, the US system of oral examination and on understanding systems seems appealing, but perhaps Airbus don't design their aircraft to be understood in quite such that manner. I don't know, I'm a Boeing driver."*
>
> *(Anonymous Pilot)*

"I do feel very strongly that robust initial training which sets high standards, combined with robust but people based checking and training is the way to build a professional pilot. I'm always skeptical of what I term 'missionary pilots' who have a mentality that is just that bit too keen. I remember my most challenging and educational training moment was in the States during initial training. An oral exam that lasted between 4-6 hours on the pa28. 4-hour sim slots and a technical exam are not of the same robustness but there has to be an atmosphere and support which aids that system."

(Anonymous Pilot)

As you will learn, the oral test the pilots speak of is no longer standard practice, but the exception. However, there is a belief that it's still occurring, or a U.S. requirement.

"The regional airline industry is an entry level industry for new pilots that graduate from schools like ERAU. Mainline carriers take the best regional Captains and military pilots so they don't have the same new hire safety issues that regional airlines have. Safety is at its most risky point during a new hire's first year or first 500 hours. During this time, it's good to have the new hire pilot use the AP as much as possible because it will teach him/her how to fly the aircraft through AP demonstration and recognize the different automation modes."

(Anonymous Pilot)

Not to disagree with the above statement regarding risk in the first 500 hours. That is a statement of fact. However, mainline carriers do not necessarily take the "best regional Captains and military pilots." There is no assessment to determine who is the best pilot. Companies select individuals they believe to best fit their culture, which may or may not be the best pilot or even the pilot with the most experience.

Overconfidence and complacency have also been associated with automation complexity—the greater the confidence in automation, the more complacent pilots may become. However, overconfidence, while it may be a predictor of behavior, does not necessarily dictate complacency.[193] A higher workload due to weather, distractions, or fatigue, are also contributing factors to pilots' reliance upon equipment during task-saturated situations. While automation usage due to situational factors may be the reason pilots opt to use higher levels of automation, the question might be asked if situational usage would create reliance and complacency, or if higher level of trust in automation versus personal ability caused that dependency.

4. Trust and Complacency

Trust but verify—words pilots live by.

TRUST IN AUTOMATION has also been identified as a determinant of automation usage—the more trust the pilot has in the automation, the more likely the pilot is to use it. Whereas early automation research attempted to understand why pilots were reluctant to fully utilize the automated equipment, the challenge shifted to understanding pilots' over-reliance on automation usage in part due to trust in the reliability of equipment. The history of automation-induced complacency identifies that higher equipment reliability led to higher complacency.[13] Due to this high reliability of current technology, many pilots now have greater trust in the equipment than they have in their ability to manually fly.

"I recently started flying long haul with pilots that are about to retire and they just don't want any sort of trouble. In 9 months flying the 787 only last Monday I got to fly with a Captain that allowed me to disconnect both the AP and AT above 10,000. Many times I've been told "this aircraft is not designed to be hand flown." I would hand fly every approach in VMC with the AP and AT off, however I usually fly with this sort of Captain."

(Anonymous Pilot)

There are a variety of operational concerns with automation usage, from over-involvement with automation at the sacrifice of primary flight situation awareness (SA), lack of understanding, over-reliance, and complacency. While the FAA has encouraged pilots to manually fly, pilots continue to be automation dependent, and reluctant to manually fly their aircraft, which has impacted performance and resulted in flight skill loss.

"Automation dependency poses a major problem nowadays. How many of us can fly a straight and level unaccelerated flight without AP, AT, and FDs?? In my company very few fly without FDs, since it's a trigger on OFDM when you turn them off. However, some procedures require them to be turned off/recycled, such as non-precision or circling. Also, very few pilots (there are over 4000 pilots in my company) do visual approaches, only because they are not sure how to execute them properly. Company's mantra has scared them and thus they lost their confidence."

(Anonymous Pilot)

With automation engaged, pilots are required to monitor aircraft displays to ensure navigation accuracy, speed, altitude, and maintain system awareness. When the automation is working changes are unexpected because the automation is maintaining programed parameters. However, monitoring challenges continue to plague automation usage as automation reliance often leads to complacency. There appears to be an innate difficulty for pilots to maintain continued focus in the presence of highly reliable equipment.[32] It's extremely difficult to focus on something that is unchanging. Despite the difficulty in maintaining continued vigilance and focus, pilots' cognitive state of trust in automation will influence their choice in levels of automation and associated automation dependence.

> *"This reliance [or overreliance] on automation seems to have made pilots complacent in their monitoring duties, in some cases, not understanding or comprehending what IS actually happening and the expected results."*
>
> (Anonymous Pilot)

5. LEVELS OF AUTOMATION

"Automation is safer that manual flight"
(Anonymous Pilot)

L EVELS OF AUTOMATION and pilot interaction have been the subject of much research. The effort was in an attempt to understand what level of automation would best support attention and focus. Pilot awareness measurement testing was conducted to better understand the relationship between levels of automation and airline pilots' task-related and task-unrelated thought patterns. Results identified that higher levels of aircraft automation enabled pilots to shift attention to higher-level flight related thought processes pertaining to flight operations.[32] An example of this would be during a complex approach, or perhaps an emergency, where thoughts beyond basic flight are necessary. Yet during a high automation and low task environment, such as enroute for many hours, pilots' minds wandered away from the flight. Challenges with lack of understanding—how to operate the automation while attempting to solve programming issues— shifted pilots' attention toward operational concerns. This shift further removed attention from the overall flight, lowering situation awareness.

Better situation awareness was identified to be present during intermediate levels of automation versus higher levels.[136] However, researchers argued that while a fully automated aircraft removes the pilot from direct control, which may result in lower situation awareness, the benefit of high automation is that cognitive overload will be reduced. Reduced cognitive overload supports improved information processing which, in turn, will enable pilots to better manage the overall operation.

"The main problem in commercial Aviation is the lack of skill and training in manual flight and when to decide reversing to manual in case of not understanding automation or in case of emergency. with ATQP it is now possible to ask for manual training during Sim session."

(Anonymous Pilot)

"Regarding the company requirements of automation usage… my current company talks about using and not using it. Whereas when I worked for a company in China, they wanted the automation on ASAP and off when [after] landing. Different mindsets… also explains why some of the Asiatic countries can't fly a visual approach to save their lives… literally. The other issue is that they are exposed to only a couple hundred hours of hand flying and then that's it."

(Anonymous Pilot)

6. EQUIPMENT FAILURE

"Unfortunately, it's [automation usage] also a double edged sword isn't it? It keeps pilots within a safety margin in day to day dealings however whenever a failure occurs it's twice as dangerous as it could potentially be because many pilots have no experience flying an approach in a jet without any automation...!"

(Anonymous Pilot)

WHAT CAN GO wrong? Go wrong? Go wrong? The reality is that equipment breaks. When it does, will the pilot be ready? Air Transat Flight 236—an Airbus A330 lost thrust in both engines due to a fuel leak. Researchers, however, attributed the pilots' reaction to the absence of integrated information within the engine, absence of fuel parameters, missing indications from traditional planes such as a yoke tilt with fuel out of balance, and purported that fuel available at *each* waypoint was hidden within the computer, as contributing factors.[54] These researchers blamed the equipment failure, due to pertinent information embedded within the flight management system, as the cause of the accident. The FAA further attributed the cause, in part, to the fuel leak itself, and recommended warning systems to alert the crew to an increase in fuel burn rate.[82]

The Air Transat Flight 236 incident presents a poignant example of a mishandled event after a system failure that was attributed to confusion, distraction, and lack of understanding. The pilots of Air Transat Flight 236 became distracted due to low oil temperature, low oil quantity, and high oil pressure. The fuel imbalance warning, designed to activate at 6,000-pound difference between wings, was the crew's first indication of a fuel leak. The crew performed a fuel balancing procedure from memory and failed to check the total fuel prior to opening crossfeed valves (a system enabling fuel to flow from one tank to the other), as directed per Airbus procedures. By opening the crossfeed valves the crew sent the fuel under pressure to the engine with the leak. The pilots reacted with the fuel out of balance warning and jumped to a procedure without first assessing the total fuel. The pilots' reaction (startle factor) to the unexpected event (automation surprise) has been identified as one of the most difficult challenges in training.[153]

> *"A working knowledge of airplane systems is an important part of training, however, you will agree with me that "trouble shooting outside the scope of the problem at hand" is NOT recommended when an issue arises on board. Pilots are trained and expected to FOLLOW published procedures as contained in the QRH [Quick Reference Handbook] or on the ECL [Electronic Checklists] as displayed on EICAS. To know what to do if there was no EICAS or CHECK-LIST would be a BIG problem in today's airplanes."*
>
> *(Anonymous Pilot)*

Lack of mode awareness is an industry concern indicating pilots are unaware of system changes, automation degradation, or decrease in performance. The inability to identify excessive fuel loss on an Airbus A330 indicates lack of system display awareness, as total fuel is always displayed on the engine page during cruise, despite researchers suggesting the fuel information was buried deep within the computers. Lack of systems understanding with low oil temperature and high oil pressure led to distraction, whereas information was available to identify a fuel leak, primarily 6000 pounds of missing fuel on the total fuel indicator.[82]

While it may not be possible to train for every potential situation, pilots must be trained to identify failures and manage the aircraft performance. They must also possess tools and skills for intervention strategies. Equipment is fallible, and when it fails pilots should have the knowledge, awareness, and ability to fly the aircraft to safety. The Air Transat pilots' ability to fly the aircraft as a glider and safely land without engines further supports the necessity for manual flight skills. A perfectly good airplane can be managed by a poorly trained pilot. An excellent pilot can fly a broken airplane. What happens when the poorly trained pilot meets the broken airplane?

I can't help to mention the Air France 447 crash in this section.[19] This Airbus A330 that initially lost all flight instruments while the pilots were in instrument conditions, which resulted in the plane falling into the ocean due to improper response. The questions is—*did the broken equipment cause the accident or did lack of understanding in how to respond to the failure cause the crash?* I contend the root cause was a safety culture issue due to lack of information sharing. The FAA and at least one international airline knew of multiple events with the same failure, yet the financial decision was to do nothing because nobody had died.

"Two airlines that have a clear policy against the regular practice of manual flight, have both come very close to crashes due to loss of control in flight (failing to understand what the automation was doing, or failing to manually recover the aircraft from an undesired state)."

(Anonymous Pilot)

Failure identification, failure recovery, and unanticipated events have been associated with automation failure. Yet, highly reliable, technologically advanced aircraft, combined with low pilot error rates, have generated challenges in legitimizing predictive models to gauge the difference between conditional pilot consequential errors or consequential errors attributed to technology. What this means is it's difficult to determine if the errors are a consequence of the technology.[264]

Research has focused on automation side effects in areas concerning complacency, bias, surprise, and mental models resulting in cognitive skill decline impacting situation awareness. Skill degradation is an interesting concept, which may be misunderstood, in that one must begin with skills prior to losing them. Training methodologies may be leaving pilots short on understanding and knowledge in the automated aircraft, without adequate time to practice flight skills. Current training may also be resulting in pilots' reluctance to manually fly their aircraft which results in flight skill loss, thus impacting multiple aspects of performance.

7. Performance

*"Honestly, from what I've seen, the basics are often
overlooked. Once I was told that a plane is just a plane.
I've carried that through training with several of my type
ratings. Maintaining the basics of flying has made each
type easier to handle. Understanding certain principals,
pitch and power, descent planning, over all hand flying on
good days, has made me exponentially better on bad days.*

*"I appreciate the levels of automation far more now
that I use them in what I feel is a proper way. Some fun-
damentals are lost in training events, because it's assumed
that you should have them at this level. It's not always the
case and they are perishable. In extreme events, it could
even have devastating results when pilots are assumed to be
proficient at flying. After all, we do it day in and day out."*

(Anonymous Pilot)

PILOT PERFORMANCE AND human factors have been the
core of research for decades. The Aviation Safety Reporting
System (ASRS) has provided the FAA with data identifying
causal factors. Yet incidents continue to occur with thousands of
ASRS reports submitted annually, reaching the millionth report

submitted in 2012.[42] These reports are the best indicators of what is happening present time. Pilots are encouraged to write a report to explain what happened and why, and they won't receive a violation unless they were negligent or the error was intentional. The system was designed to encourage pilots to come forward in order to use these reports to create a fix so the event would not be repeated. However, an administrative law judge recently conveyed his concern that he is seeing a rise in the number of reports, but the fixes are not following. The continued increase in the number of reports support his assumption.

Human error has contributed to numerous accidents where fatigue, cognitive overload, communication problems, and information processing have resulted in faulty decision-making. While decision-making can be directly connected to performance, "knowledge, skills, attitudes, systems environment, and obstacles" are essential elements of performance.[23] Performance tied to automation encompasses an extensive range of research to include manual flight, pilot error, situation awareness, decision-making, and pilot experience.

*"There are industry pilots and people who achieve to have
a License... big issue is that we stop to achieve our minimum required performance. And most people hide behind
automation and forget their obligations as pilots. Normally
I ask pilots about max crosswind limitations with or
without autopilot... curious stuff human max. Still above
auto pilot... why?! That's question. ...reply is very easy... I
barely use auto pilot on any approach ... is moment to be
in control and to make my training. ...that's why I found
curious ... ILS are authorized to 200 ft without automation as you know ... if so is because we must be able to do
... this subject apart I understand the objective of your
questions... but don't be afraid to check... you wanna
know the reality ... I think !! All Lucky. At last someone
willing to take on the Human Factor beast lurking in the
shadows, hiding behind a quick blame-the-pilot escape."*

(Anonymous Pilot)

Pilot performance in this research was identified by how the pilot
chose to operate the aircraft and associated levels of automation,
but was not measured. This research was not designed to judge how
well a pilot flew. Performance was defined as to how they chose to
operate their aircraft—manual flight or a level of automation. As
it was, results identified that performance was associated to pilot
error, accidents, major incidents, and ASRS as reported in the FAA
working group's final report of performance-based operations.[79]

8. Manual Flight

"I would fly more manually without the auto thrust if my company allowed it… shame!"

(Anonymous Pilot)

O F ALL THE performance requirements the FAA mandates of a pilot, the one that may be forgotten is the requirement to fly an airplane within required standards. Pilots are required to maintain plus or minus 100 feet, plus or minus 10 knots and have the ability to roll out of a bank within 5 degrees. The autopilot does a great job of this, but can today's pilot do the same? Despite the 2013 FAA safety alert recommending pilots manually fly their aircraft, performance assessment continues to identify that pilots are experiencing flight skill loss due lack of manual flight. Airline pilots should have both opportunity and ability to disengage the automation. However, reluctance to do so has gone unaddressed in previous research.

Human error has been a consistent factor in aviation accidents since the beginning of flight, and has directed the focus on cognitive architecture to increase safety through improved human performance. Cognitive architecture is the framework representing the mind's structures and processes, related to working memory, information processing, and long-term memory storage. Human error extends beyond mode awareness issues and automated flight confusion, to include manual aircraft handling errors. The type of errors were identified by the FAA working group to include:

+ Manual operation is difficult after transition from automated control;

+ Crew coordination problems;

+ Training is inadequate;

+ Behavior of automation, based on pilot input or other factors, may not be apparent to pilots;

+ Understanding of automation is inadequate;

+ Inadequate knowledge;

+ Cross-verification.[79]

> *"After a 30 yr. career I have observed hand flying skills deteriorate quite a bit with my first officers. However, they do an excellent job with the automation."*
>
> (Anonymous Pilot)

The working group reported that the percentages of manual handling errors where manual flight was identified as a contributing factor was in an excess of 60% of all accidents and 30% of major incidents reviewed.

"We are not allowed to disengage the autothrust at any time, no matter the circumstances. A few years ago, we lost the autothrust inflight on the A330 and even though it was a non-event, we had to file a safety report with the company. Yup, that's how bad it gets here. The flight directors have to stay on at all times as well. It's unfortunate but they do not trust us at all at this carrier."

(Anonymous Pilot)

LOSA, Flight Operations Quality Assurance (FOQA) data, Aviation Safety Reporting System (ASRS), and Aviation Safety Action Program (ASAP) reports do not provide adequate indicators of pilot procedural knowledge. Line Check Safety Audits (LCSA) would explain FOQA results, however, LOSA, FOQA, LCSA, ASAP and ASRS data do not ascertain knowledge and cannot assess hand flying performance if the pilots are utilizing automation. They also do not indicate why pilots are not hand flying, let alone identify the pilots' level of confidence in knowledge and ability.

"In [Airline] they were pro automated flights, which I think it's great when you have your manual flying background experience: that experience that takes you to disconnect and fly manually, with confidence, when the airplane is not doing what you want. And works great in airports with high density traffic. But, on the other hand, you feel you gradually lose your manual flight skills."

(Anonymous Pilot)

"Manual Flight: for me, the least I have to do is disengage the autopilot. From there on I fly the aircraft manually (at least as far as this is possible on the Airbusses ;-) I might disengage the autothrust, as well, but the boundary between auto flight and manual flight lies with the use of the autopilot."

(Anonymous Pilot)

————————

"I do not believe I saw one single question on your survey related to fatigue. Fatigue is a very serious issue for any commercial airline crew. A pilot's decision to hand-fly an aircraft will be affected by the pilot's determination of his/her physical state and the state of his/her fellow Flight Deck crew member. If the Flying Pilot (FP) is too tired, he'll more than likely allow the Autopilot (AP) to fly the aircraft."

(Anonymous Pilot)

————————

"A couple things that are unique to the Eclipse 550 (Airplane I am currently flying) that are unusual and possibly unique to the airplane. The autothrottles automatically kick off when the landing gear is lowered. The software was designed that way because they wanted the pilot "in the loop" closer to the ground."

(Anonymous Pilot)

————————

"I must say, being a former Air Force (TacHel, Ab Initio Jet Instructor, Fighters) for 20 years and showing up in the Commercial world now for 8 years, I couldn't believe how little energies are spent for hands on flying… My 3 previous aircraft all had sticks, the first 2 had no automation at all, and you would only live for about 5 secs if you let go of the cyclic on the B212… the Hornet was pretty whiz bang with level 3 automation.

"It was pretty funny and sometimes "not cool" when I would ask the Captain as a newbie FO if I could hand fly the APP or DEP all the way… it seems we have become systems managers, relying mostly on 2-3 AP to make us look good most of the time. When asked in the sim if there is something (sequences) I would like to see/do when our official script is complete, I always ask to fly a VFR circuit to a T&G, and time permitting a SE ILS APP manually to 200 & 1/2… sometimes it's nice, sometimes not so much… ha!"

(Anonymous Pilot)

9. PILOT ERROR

I F THE PILOT is always to blame, then nothing will solve the problem. Pilot error and flight skill loss have become an industry concern due to reliance on automation and lack of manual flight practice. However, research has identified that flight skill retention in automated aircraft remains relatively intact without consistent practice, yet degradation of cognitive ability necessary for manual flight was apparent.[123]

There have been suggestions, however, that pilots who pay attention to flight performance enroute with the automation engaged perform better in identifying system failures, aircraft tracking, and position awareness; more so than if ignoring the automated flight performance.[32] Thus, automation usage in itself is not performance debilitating, but is contingent upon pilot awareness and the level of attention. All errors are not the same.

Proficiency errors account for about 70% of consequential errors, while decision-making errors accounted for over 40% and communication accounted for 10% of errors.[121] Proficiency errors identify a need for technical training, necessitating more ground school training to educate pilots on systems understanding. Whereas decision-making and communication errors indicated a need for team training, as in simulator LOFT training. As identified, 30% more consequential errors occur than decision-making errors, and 60% more than communication errors. This indicates a necessity to increase technical training, and suggests a strong need to improve ground school. However, current training methodologies revolve around communication training. This type of training is (or has been) effective and poor communication is not the issue that it once was. Therefore, the industry appears to be focusing on the wrong type of training to improve operational performance.

Pilot error is a nebulous term, in that the pilots can only use the tools they were provided. Unfortunately, the industry has attributed all accidents and incidents to pilot error. While this chapter is a standalone, the reason for pilot error falls within all chapters. It's never only for one reason that a plane crashes. Pilots do not intentionally cause errors risking their lives. When pilots are not given training, are required to read and understand the systems on their own from poorly written manuals, not told of systems in the aircraft and trained for subsequent failures, or information is withheld from previous incidents, they cannot be blamed for pilot error. Situation awareness belongs in the organization as well.

10. Situation Awareness

"I had great confidence in my first officer's performance and he opted to manually fly the full arrival into Seattle. With vectors, altitude and speed constraints, and requirement to slow to 180 knots where L/D [Lift over drag] requires speed brakes to descend on profile [B777]. I have never been so busy keeping up with him. If the plane had crashed I would have been two miles behind the accident."

(Anonymous Pilot)

SITUATION AWARENESS IS a key concept in aviation, in that pilots need to be situationally aware to mitigate risk and improve operational safety. Situation awareness (SA) has been defined as "the perception of the elements in the environment within a volume of time and space, the comprehension of their meaning, and the projection of their status in the near future".[63] Inadequate SA has been attributed to 52% of all accidents and is a focus of aviation human factors research.[7] Situation awareness is also impacted by the working memory and cognitive overload.

An overloaded working memory prohibits both learning and memory formation. Yet, the automated aircraft is an integral element of the innate limitation of the working memory due to susceptibility of capacity overload as a result of large amounts of complex information. This overload in turn reduces situation awareness.

Technological advancement also enables highly complex machines to remain at altitude for extended periods of time, requiring longer periods of automation monitoring. This decreases pilot performance as sleep deprivation and mental fatigue add to cognitive overload. Dehydration, associated with long flights, further negatively impacts cognitive function and memory. The complexity of the automated aircraft, fatigue, dehydration, and external factors like inclement weather, system failures, or unexpected events impinge upon an already overloaded working memory, further reduces SA.

Automaticity has been noted as essential for airline pilots to improve SA, and lack of automaticity may limit their decision-making ability. Automaticity indicates a pilot's knowledge is at the level where he or she does not have to consciously think about what to do and the response is automatic. Over-learning to the point where the pilot becomes unconsciously competent—the pilot performs tasks without conscious thought—is a level of performance essential for aircraft operations.[23] However, concern for automaticity has not gone unnoticed in regard to reduced SA due to a perceived inability for the pilot to transfer task at hand duties to conscious thought, which are necessary to adapt to changes in the environment. Routine expertise may lead to quick and immediate reactions, that would be likened to rote memorization. However, performance in a changing environment demands a deeper level of understanding.

That deeper level of understanding is associated with adaptive expertise that will be adaptable to unique situations. That deeper level of understanding lays in adaptive expertise. Adaptive expertise requires precise knowledge, in both quality and content, to be structurally organized in the memory, as well as required for metacognitive skills necessary for *planning, monitoring, and memory.*[232] Elements of adaptive expertise, where understanding and contextual-based knowledge combined with motivation for problem solving, create more adaptive and flexible strategies for unexpected events, whereas rote memorization is limited with a new experience.[25]

The answer as to when immediate processing of automaticity would help or hinder situation awareness and ensuing performance, lies in a distinction between rote memorization versus knowledge based understanding, and routine expertise versus adaptive expertise. An unconsciously competent pilot's performance would be associated with automaticity and adaptive expertise. This is different from rote memorization which is associated with routine experience. Automaticity and adaptive expertise improve performance during novel situations. Rote memorization results in limited understanding and memorized procedures may not transfer to the aircraft beyond events practiced and anticipated in the simulator. Rote memorization also does not guarantee the pilot understands the automatic response, whereas knowledge-based automaticity and adaptive expertise imply a deeper level of understanding that could be critical to the safe operation of a flight.

"In regard to systems knowledge, I think the pendulum has swung to rote and saying what the switch does but that's not to say I need to know how many holes are drilled around the edge of the static port. The studying was pretty easy since we had a study guide and the instructors could only ask questions out of the systems bank. But the toughest part of all this is finding experienced people who can help because a third of [Airline] pilots are new hire FO's. We'll figure it out one way or another!"

(Anonymous Pilot)

———————

Research further identified that pilots with a more developed information processing ability and working memory improved their situation awareness and performance with higher levels of automation.[133] The reverse was true for pilots with lower levels of information processing ability and working memory. Yet, during periods of high workload, higher levels of automation usage has been known to improve situation awareness. However, when mental workload is increased due to lack of understanding of complex aircraft systems, operations, or interpreting the automation, higher levels of automation will reduce situation awareness if the pilot is mentally overloaded.

"The aircraft I fly has AP and AT and it's definitely a mood or fatigue feeling regarding the disengagement of them individually or all off, and since we get worked like ragged dogs the automation is used a lot… not ALL the time but a lot.

"I've found nearly everyone with the automation disengaged keeps the flight director on at all times as it still provides a relevant source of direction, turn source, etc. Another factor in disengagement of the automation depends on the environment flown into—not just weather specific but airspace/type of flying specific. I'm more likely going to hand fly into Jackson Hole in VMC than I would into LAX unless I'm behind a heavy for example."

(Anonymous Pilot)

A European research project, Enhanced Safety through Situation Awareness Integration in Training (ESSAI), assessed the impact of SA in relation to airline accidents and incidents. The results identified that flight crews improved SA with ESSAI training, beyond FAA approved LOFT scenarios.[15] LOFT, an AQP requirement, was developed to integrate Crew Resource Management (CRM) as a risk mitigation process for pilot error based upon communication strategies. However, ESSAI training showed improvements above LOFT training in cognitive efficiency, automaticity and interpersonal dynamics subscales. It also improved judgment assessment, increased flexibility with a changing environment, and improved memory for routine performance.

With all the lessons learned about situation awareness, it becomes interesting how this concept has transferred into the corporate side of the house. Management should also identify a situation, comprehend the meaning, and the project the status into the future. This is the essence of risk mitigation. Different from pilots, managers have time in a safe quiet space to analyze the situation and determine the best outcome. Unfortunately, those decisions appear to become financially driven.

Whether automation improves or reduces situation awareness with the pilot is dependent upon the pilot's cognitive ability and the level of overload under a given situation. Cognitive overload is not isolated, but also susceptible to multiple and changing environmental factors that could impact decision-making.

11. DECISION-MAKING

E VERY PILOT KNOWS that good decisions come from experience, and experience comes from bad decisions.

The success of a flight is the result of all decisions. Two different cognitive processing styles have been identified with decision-making—analytical and non-analytical. Analytical processing is noted to be slower, more elaborative, requires more cognitive effort, and derives more conscious ability. Non-analytical decision-making is quicker, takes less cognitive effort and is often accomplished without a conscious effort. Captain Sullenberger's decision to land in the Hudson River (US Airways Flight 1549), was due to his perception of the inability to make a runway. It was not based upon analytical calculations but an implicit knowledge, based on extensive experience. Intuitive problem solving research has identified that implicit knowledge, such as Captain Sullenberger's experience, was based upon unconscious perception related to perception structure, learning, decision-making, and problem solving.[210]

Information processing is a key component of decision-making when a pilot must choose between options. The process includes both environment assessment and *cue seeking*. Cue seeking is the process of searching for environment cues pertinent to the situation.

Without adequate SA—a lack of perception of the environment, lack of comprehension or understanding of what is being observed or experienced, and projection into the future—the pilot may be challenged in making informed decisions. Decision-making represents the third stage in Wickens' human information processing model (HIP)—after stimuli and perception—and is followed by execution and feedback.[264] The decision is determined by understanding the situation and all elements relative to that situation.

Without adequate knowledge, understanding, or experience, decisions may be based on (a) satisficing, where the pilot takes the first available option, (b) a naturalistic decision based on feeling of familiarity, or (c) heuristics, a mental shortcut associated with cognitive overload. If the Air France pilots from Flight 447 had knowledge that the pitot system was prone to failure and had been trained how to manage the aircraft—228 people could be alive today. If the FAA required redundant systems, or the FAA and Boeing had mandated a new type-rating on the B737 MAX— 346 people would be alive. If Atlas Air heeded the research that many of their pilots lacked understanding, 3 pilots would be alive. Accidents don't only destroy the lives on the plane, but also lives of the people that were connected to them.

While experience is an essential component of both problem solving and decision-making, experience must be in the context of deliberate practice versus routine performance.[252]

12. EXPERIENCE

"Required training for pilots seems to have been reduced in terms of flight time and with the introduction of the Multi Pilot License, (MPL), actual real world experience has also been cut down to simulator training time."

(Anonymous Pilot)

TO PUT FLIGHT time into perspective—is 1,500 hours equal to one hour of experience 1,500 times, or 1,500 hours of actual experience? If the industry simply looks at numbers as the flight time requirement, they may be forcing companies to employ the least experienced pilot due to supply and demand. The only pilots employable are those with 1500 hours. However, five hundred hours of actual experience flying in South East Alaska could be more valuable than 1 hour of experience in traffic pattern 1500 times.

Researchers investigated how pilots retain and learn skills while flying. It's been determined, that the level of practice and training during daily flight and the time elapsed since initial flight training, significantly influences airline pilots' fine-motor flying skills.[117] In addition to frequency and time, the frequency of when and how knowledge is used has also been identified as a key factor in pilot performance. However, automated aircraft provide limited opportunities for knowledge application beyond procedural knowledge. There is also no requirement for knowledge assessment during pilot recency, or recurrent training events beyond rote memorization of limitations or memory items, and no requirements for repetition or practice of manual flight skills.

> *"I'm a Flight Instructor on the A320 and believe manual flight is a lost art. I get crews to practice as often as the weather allows. Either manual thrust or Autopilot off F/D off and when comfortable all three. Ground courses are too short, SIM's are tick the box regulatory exercises and don't give the crew time to practice, practice, practice. I believe over learning is the key, I'd like to say that's my idea, but I can't.*
>
> *"Another sad thing is I sometime feel like I am the "alien" and no one else see the pattern. Maybe it shows my age."*
>
> (Anonymous Pilot)

———————

Competency requires practice via repetition, feedback as to the success and/or failure of the pilot's performance, and confidence that performance will result in a safe outcome. Repetition for performance cannot be overstressed as it leads to unconscious competency, a state where overlearning, automaticity, and adaptive expertise improve situation awareness and overall performance. Repetition and practice are necessary to take a pilot from novice to expert, yet the transition to expert could take up to *ten years of practice*.[241] Malcolm Gladwell professed that it took 10,000 hours to become an expert in his book *Outliers*. The concern is that pilots may not be getting the required practice to become an expert in manual flight.

Furthermore, current AQP mandates do not require pilots to see most Terminal Proficiency Objective (TPO) events more than once in the simulator, and many pilots may go years, if ever, prior to experiencing the actual event. TPOs are the "statements of performance, conditions, and standards established at the task level" written as AQP directives of training.[86]

The nature of long-haul flying and aircraft complexity has also created unique challenges in the areas of pilot competency and performance. The challenge to gain experience in highly automated aircraft is that they can stay airborne longer than 16 hours. Therefore, long-haul pilots experience fewer opportunities for repetition and practice of manual flight skills. Long-haul flights also demand multiple pilots due to the length of flight time; yet, only one pilot conducts the takeoff and landing event. This prevents three of the four pilots from having the opportunity to gain experience or maintain currency. Flight time no longer equals experience. In addition, fifty percent of the flight time, with a crew of four, will be in a crew-rest facility.

Reduced vertical separation minimums (RVSM) require autopilot use enroute, thus further eliminating opportunities for manual flight. As opposed to domestic flying, many long-haul pilots also visit a simulator every 90-days, per Federal Aviation Regulation (FAR) 121.439, to obtain three takeoffs and landings. Yet these pilots meet only minimum requirements during this currency event to make them *legal* to fly. Thus, pilots have little opportunity during training or line flying to work toward higher levels of expertise.

Performance is based on proficient operating skills in a simulator, thus the only place to gain expertise is on the flight line. However, flight line operations utilize a fraction of the functionality of highly automated aircraft under normal operations. Therefore, pilots are challenged with the ability to gain a level of confidence in systems knowledge and operations beyond the minimum without experiencing operations in the simulator.

An Airbus Industries senior vice president of engineering stated, "FMC's [Flight Management Computers] may offer too many possibilities and be too complex, with the result that many pilots rely on only 20% of the software features."[228]

"A very interesting topic—I could talk for hours about automation, the modern flight deck, training and engagement with the aircraft being flown. Having raced around with my hair on fire in Royal Air Force fast jets, flown pretty much all the Airbus types and now the B787-9 I hope I would not be bragging to say I've experienced a wide variety of flying. The biggest problem I see these days is a real reluctance to disengage the automatics (autopilot, autothrust and FD) due to company policy but primarily lack of confidence due, in my opinion, to lack of practice.

"When flying with the automatics most pilots are not fully 'engaged' with what the a/c is doing but when you are hand flying it you are 'engaged' because you are physically 'putting the a/c where you want it'. I hear all too often these days my F/O say can he hand fly the approach because he has his sim check coming up and wants to practice—isn't that the wrong way around??? LOL but a serious point."

(Anonymous Pilot)

Company policy is also impacting pilot experience by mandating automation usage. A professor queried me in his assumption that operators demanded higher levels of automation usage for fuel efficiencies. While automation usage could maximize fuel efficiencies during enroute flight segments, decision making and flight management has the greater impact on fuel. Decision-making regarding cruise altitudes, speed, descent planning, gear and flap extension, speedbrake usage, and the ability to fly an on-profile approach, will all impact fuel efficiencies that are in control of the pilot, regardless of the level of automation. One missed approach due to poor planning will cost thousands in added fuel expense.

Most importantly, flight hours in automated aircraft do not improve aircraft systems knowledge, and they do not increase pilot performance when an unanticipated event occurs. It's been suggested that a typical pilot spends less than two-minutes per flight segment manually flying. While the Federal Aviation Regulation (FAR) 121.439 requires pilots to have three takeoffs and landings in 90 days to maintain currency, some pilots may go many months without ever seeing the inside of the flight deck of an actual aircraft due to a reserve system, where the pilot is on call and not flying.

Despite the three takeoffs and landings requirement in 90 days, there are no requirements for normal operations to conduct a pre-flight, practice in-flight operational procedures (normal, abnormal, or emergency), perform navigation tasks, or fly a takeoff or descent profile during a recency event. In addition, there is no requirement to demonstrate operational competency beyond takeoffs and landing proficiency that may be performed with the autopilot and autothrust engaged, or systems knowledge assessment.

Mandates for manual flight during initial flight training for departures and arrivals went into effect in 2019, yet there are no requirements for recency training, indicating this may be a one-time event. To gain the benefits of this training, practice must prevail. Performance based upon greater operational experience would also improve confidence.

> *"Most pilots at my company will elect to turn the autopilot off once within 1000-500' of the runway in visual conditions. I almost always have it off by the 1000' callout. Auto throttles are usually left on until 30' with most pilots. I've only ever seen 1 or 2 pilots do a visual approach with no AP, no AT and no FD at my airline. It's extremely frowned upon at our company especially since the level of experience is starting to get lower and lower with the pilot shortage."*
>
> *(Anonymous Pilot)*

> *"I have been an instructor at both airlines I have worked at: [Airline A] and [Airline B].*
>
> *"[Airline A] I was a line check pilot and usually the last chance guy. [Airline B] I was an instructor on the 744 in the sim and now on the 767 as a line check pilot. Both were appendix F training places. Being that both aren't places that pilots dreamed working at, I have seen a wide swath in initial qualifications as well as high turnover and a dilution of culturally ingrained techniques. Obviously, one had schedules of high flight cycles and the other is extremely low cycles. I have found extremely surprising similar weaknesses in both types of flying. The three main weakness being: mode confusion, knowing when to use what level of automation, and recognizing red flags of task saturation in early stages.*

"I see you flew the Classic as well. When we parked them, I was surprised how well people that had flown steam for 40 years tend to adapt. There were outliers, but the vast majority picked it up well. The odd thing I found was that on the 744, with our FAR minimum training at 6 and 12 month sim visits was that the vast majority could fly the plane quite well when it was the silly OEI hand-flown ILS. You would still see pilots who flew the plane for a decade struggle with using the automation in normal, or slightly abnormal (leveling under 10k if a door pops) situation.

"It was odd. The pilot stuff one does every six months was actually way better than expected. Probably a ramble, but I find this subject fascinating. I could go on for days."

(Anonymous Pilot)

13. Confidence

CONFIDENCE THAT CORRESPONDS with competence is related to operational success and resultant safety. Confidence is critical to operational safety and efficiency, however, overconfidence has the opposite effect. The FAA working group found that over-reliance in automation attributed to numerous accidents, incidents and ASRS reports. They further reported that pilots' overconfidence in automation was a contributing factor to one-quarter of the accidents reviewed. Overconfidence in automation was correlated with pilots' lack of confidence in their own ability, suggesting that they were more comfortable using the automation than taking manual control.[79]

Confidence has not only been associated with performance, but is an integral component of the learning process. Pilots must feel confident that their level of performance will ensure a safe operation.[134] The pilot personality is one that innately exudes confidence, and to the benefit of safety. The higher confidence level enables pilots to deal more effectively with higher amounts of stress than less confident individuals.[46] However, if a pilot does not understand the operation of their aircraft, the added stress and associated reduction in confidence impacts their ability to perform and willingness to manually fly the aircraft.

Whereas confidence is essential to positive performance, overconfidence may push pilots into more risky behavior with a feeling of infallibility. Thus, training programs should focus on teaching pilots to control the aircraft, not making them falsely overconfident.[20] Overconfidence has been defined as a high-risk employee trait. While overconfidence has been a topic of research, current training programs are doing nothing to build confidence. The lack of understanding and inability to practice are actually creating a lack of confidence, as is the lack of manual flight.

Corroborative research further discovered that, "People tend to attribute positive experiences to things that are permanent and to attribute negative experiences to transient effects".[41] Thus, a pilot who passes a check ride may attribute success to their ability. The pilot who fails the checking event may blame the simulator not being representative of the aircraft, blame the supporting pilot for errors made, or blame the instructor's lack of ability—transient experiences. It's been identified that success is predictive of future success, whereas failures have no predictive impact.[41] However, success and failure may shift a pilot's level of confidence without substantiated performance to support their belief.

Confidence also affects the operator's decision to utilize automation. When pilots trust the automation more so than their own ability, they become more dependent upon the automation. Pilots' higher level of confidence in their ability, more so than the automation they are more apt to disengage the automation and manually fly. Pilots' confidence in their ability further influences their decision-making and reactions during anticipated and actual experiences with the environment. Self-efficacy is identified as the individual's belief in their ability to create the desired results. The greater the pilots' perceived self-efficacy, the greater their performance as well as their persistence to succeed.[16] Self-efficacy identifies a person's belief in his or her ability to perform.

A study of United Kingdom glass-cockpit pilots' attitudes toward automation showed that pilots generally believed they had a good level of understanding of the aircraft and its systems and further believed that automation increased their confidence.[172] However, as pointed out in this study, that despite pilots' confidence on understanding systems the lack of awareness and lack of aircraft understanding may only become apparent during a catastrophic failure.

A 1997 study of multidimensional theory of cognitive (mental) anxiety, somatic (physical) anxiety, and self-confidence with Tae Kwon-Do athletes during competition had interesting results regarding the power of confidence. Results indicated that the best performers had higher self-confidence scores and lower cognitive and somatic anxiety scores than the lower performers. Another key point of this study was that 63% of the athletes were correctly predicted as winners based upon their scores with self-confidence the highest factor.[35]

A 2005 study used 1200 decision-based questions to study confidence, performance development, and the correlation between the two. Findings identified that confidence develops gradually, does not develop at the same rate as performance, develops at a diminishingly increasing rate dependent, in part, upon the nature of the task, and develops as a function of positive and negative feedback.[91]

*"In real-life, confidence often serves as
a proxy for, or a predictor of expertise,
performance, and competency."*
(Fischer and Budescu)

Beyond confidence in operational performance, pilots' confidence that they understand the aircraft systems may be overestimated as to their actual understanding and they may be operationally proficient, yet unconsciously incompetent.[23] Meaning, they don't know what they don't know.

14. Understanding

"I believe there will be a generation of pilots that will understand nothing about how their aircraft truly work and I believe this will lead to a loss of life. The final report, as you've said, will blame the pilot."

(Anonymous Pilot)

PILOTS ARE TRAINED and expected to *follow* published procedures as contained in the QRH (Quick Reference Handbook) or on the ECL (Electronic Checklists) as displayed on EICAS (Engine Indication and Crew Alerting System). To know what to do if there was no EICAS or checklist would be a big problem in today's airplanes. Understanding has been the one consistent theme throughout the history of aviation accidents, incidents, and reports—yet training has not been adequately addressed.

The FAA working group analysis reported a knowledge deficiency, in some capacity, attributed to over 40% of the accidents and 30% of major incidents they reviewed, and LOSA narratives identified that flight path errors were due to knowledge deficit and automation usage.[79]

"I would say automation dependency is becoming prevalent, and there will be a generation of pilots who do not

know the pitch thrust relationship for their aircraft. One specific example comes to mind, while flying as a captain on the E175 at [Airline], I first placed my hand in front of the N1 gauges at cruise, then asked the FO what he thought it should be roughly.

"He answered honestly saying he had no idea, but then I told him to take a guess, he said maybe 65%. We were closer to 87%, and I was hoping he'd say 85-90%, so I told him it was higher, then uncovered the gauges. It really drove the point home, and he acknowledged that he should have a better idea. I should add at [Airline] now there is very much a culture of leave everything on—even though the book allows for disconnecting everything to stay proficient.

"When I have hand flown, or offered to let the FO hand fly, on a VFR day in a low workload environment, they seem timid at first. Which brings me to another story, I flew with a different FO from my first story, and he was surprised that I wanted to let him turn everything off (AT, AP, FD). At first, I gave him guidance on what to do, but as he flew, he got more proficient and realized how his skills needed to be used so that he would not regress. During upgrade training, I made the suggestion that there should be more emphasis on the pitch + power/thrust relationship, as a few months prior a crew disengaged the AT in a descent, but did not bring thrust back up. They got the shaker over Santa Monica coming into LAX. I am glad they recovered, but I feel if they were prepared to set a N1 for the desired airspeed, it would have been a much better outcome."

(Anonymous Pilot)

"Given recent accidents like Asiana in SFO, or Emirates in DXB emphasizes the importance of not only monitoring, but making adjustments if the automation is not doing what it should, or what the pilots want. Interestingly the children of the magenta [line] uses the phrase click, click (AP)...click, click (AT) to describe this. If the automation does not give the desired reaction, pilots can still manipulate the controls to do so which is our job at the end of the day."

(Anonymous Pilot)

———————

Since the 1996 human factors team report, equipment and procedural changes have addressed mode awareness and flight management computer (FMC) operation. Yet lack of understanding as to what the displayed information means and operational programming errors continue to be industry issues. If pilots do not have a solid understanding of their aircraft, with both cognitive and physical skills, the added challenges of NextGen may increase that level of instability with added distractions and increased workload. In the simplest terms, NexGen is where satellite-based systems will replace ground-based systems for air traffic management, and will increase pilots' operational requirements.

"I frequently observe the absolutely worst scenario: use of automation by pilots who don't possess full understanding of the FMS/FMA/AT relationship. To exacerbate the problem, verbal FMA annunciations are not required by our manuals, so errors are plentiful. It saddens to see how young men and women who were flight instructors in their recent past become willing slaves to the flight director and forget all about primary instrumentation scan! It scares me when I think of those pilots being forced to execute a manual go-around in IMC and/or at night, immediately envisioning recent horrific accidents in my native Russia and other parts of the world that were caused by the somatogravic illusion, illusions in particular and by degradation of instrument scanning skills in general."

(Anonymous Pilot)

History has also shown that when new technology is introduced a period of instability develops associated with the learning curve, which creates an environment open for catastrophe. This learning curve has everything to do with the level of understanding, and associated operational use. Imagine the first time you utilized a computer, switched from a PC to a MAC, or your company changed operational programs, and the number of errors made. The working group identified 10% of major incidents, 22% of accidents, 25% of LOSA events and 35% of ASRS incidents were due to FMS programming errors, and 25% of accidents were due to mode selection errors.

"Safety is a great subject and a not negotiable element in aviation. I have a very interesting incident that happened to me in London on… and the lack of understanding of safety by certain airlines is just mind boggling to say the least!"

(Anonymous Pilot)

———————

An investigation of 336 ASRS incident reports between June 2009 and May 2014 focused on pilot confusion.[213] Previous research was utilized identifying two types of confusion.[214] Type 1 was based on cognitive function, where the pilot did not understand the experience. Type 2 was based upon behavior that resulted in confusion, such as reading a wrong checklist and confusing the other pilot. The implication of these studies was that in 1993 pilots were "1.32 times more likely to report Type 1 than Type 2 confusion, whereas the current results indicated reports of Type 1 increased to 1.96 times more likely than Type 2."[213] This indicates that lack of understanding—where pilots are more confused overall—has increased more than behavior-based confusion. In 1993, pilots reported confusion as a contributing factor in 1 of 10 aviation safety reports.

AQP training focused on Crew Resource Management (CRM) and communication to eliminate pilot error, yet, two decades later confusion has become the most reported factor in aviation accidents and incidents. This type of confusion is directly related to cognitive function and lack of systems understanding, which has been a long standing problem yet to be addressed. Multiple characteristics of confusion include:

➤ cognitive-based, associated with feelings of uncertainty

✦ appraisal-based reacting to, and in conflict with, the environment

✦ subjective involving knowledge and understanding

✦ both an authentic emotion and a subjective experience[213]

Lack of understanding may be an overlooked characteristic leading to confusion, where confusion is defined as, "A situation in which people are uncertain about what to do or are unable to understand something clearly, and the feeling that you have when you do not understand what is happening, what is expected, etc."[43] The underlying reasons for lack of understanding were examined, and identified that knowledge inadequacy related to whether or not the knowledge had been in the first place. In addition, how often the knowledge was used, if the pilot received feedback as to their level of knowledge, and issues related to training such as, training curriculum relevance, learning methodologies, compatibility with the organization, and the pilot's aptitude toward learning also impacted understanding.[23] To assess pilot knowledge, the following eight questions were recommended to identify if the pilot was unconsciously incompetent, lacking awareness of the experience:

✦ What are the observable facts concerning crew knowledge?

✦ Could the crew comprehend the situation that was occurring?

✦ Could the crew select a reasonable strategy from a set of strategies?

✦ Was the crew aware of all reasonable alternatives?

✦ Did the crew know how to choose alternatives?

✈ Was the crew aware of the consequences of the available alternatives?

✈ Did the crew have knowledge to carry out the chosen strategy?

✈ Could the crew assess the system response to the chosen strategy?[23]

> *"Systems was a "memorize the book take a computer test and regurgitate information" and then the oral was on limitations, also memorized for that event. Nobody really asked me anything to see if I understood the aircraft or how it operated."*
>
> *(Anonymous Pilot)*

In 2011 Captain Wise conducted a descriptive study during his doctoral research to assess airline pilot knowledge at Atlas airlines. Atlas operates the Boeing B747-400, B747-8, and B767-200/300 aircraft—all automated, glass cockpit, aircraft. The sample included 321 pilots, and results indicated that *two thirds* of those pilots were below an 80% knowledge level, with very few demonstrating proficiency greater than the 90% level after training. More than half the pilots exhibited substandard performance with mode awareness and changes in automation. These findings of limited knowledge and weakness in identifying mode changes parallel challenges at the time of this research, with lack of understanding and confusion.

In 2019 Atlas Flight 3591 experienced a catastrophic accident killing all onboard due to pilot confusion after the crew inadvertently bumped the TOGA switch that placed the aircraft into a go-around mode.[275] These pilots failed to recognize a mode change, did not disengage the autopilot to regain control, lacked understanding as how to control the aircraft, and crashed.

Early researchers purported that if pilots understood how the automation worked, they would have a greater ability to use it correctly.[194] That contention has not changed, but nothing has been done to address the problem. In 2007, research identified inadequate training and guidance resulting in insufficient knowledge and experience as causal factors in 19 airline accidents.[58] Five years later researchers expanded upon factors that contributed to the lack of understanding with automated systems, to include system complexity, interface design, and substandard training.[66] Unfortunately, worldwide regulators have allowed airlines to reduce training, eliminate it in some cases, and expect pilots to teach themselves at home. Despite the preponderance of information that points a finger at inadequate training to be the culprit of aviation accidents and incidents, training footprints have been reduced with FAA approval.

An additional problem with reduced understanding, even when the system is operating normally, is that it diminishes situation awareness. Without knowledge and understanding it would be difficult, if not impossible, for a pilot to comprehend the situation of what is happening (Level 2 SA) in order to project the situation into the future (Level 3 SA), thus reducing performance.[66] Pilots worldwide may be deficient in knowledge of the aircraft they fly, which under normal operations may manifest in a safe outcome. However, when the unusual occurs, the unexpected event may instigate an inappropriate reaction.

"There is no "oral" as part of a proficiency check. Depending on the operator, there may be a few questions prior to the ride, but usually it's just to discuss the profile and then get in the sim and go do it.

"I do feel very strongly that robust initial training which sets high standards, combined with robust but people based checking and training is the way to build a professional pilot. I remember my most challenging and educational training moment was in the States during initial training. An oral exam that lasted between 4-6 hours on the PA28.

"Company culture and welfare toward pilots are more important. Manual flight is a basic concept but automation is kind of trend! Especially long distance flight and automation is kind of trend! Especially long distance flight and auto flight are well connected all the time. After all the that's why we need simulator training twice a year."

(Anonymous Pilot)

———————

The Air France Flight 447 accident presents a poignant example of confusion and lack of systems and performance knowledge. The crew's inappropriate response indicated the pilots were consciously incompetent, aware of the gravity of the situation, yet unable to solve the problem. Some researchers have argued that Air France Flight 447 crashed as a result of cognitive processes contrary to lack of knowledge.[205] Yet, cognitive overload and working memory challenges have been attributed to knowledge transfer and long-term memory, impacting knowledge acquisition. Research further indicates that the majority of pilots may not fully understand complete FMC functionality and operational modes, and recommends the solution is a focus on training.[189] Research has now identified that lack of understanding is impacting the pilots' decision to manually fly. Pilots' lack of understanding aircraft systems and operations may be a direct result of poor or inadequate pilot training.

15. Training

"Unfortunately, today's training environment is too centered (in my opinion) on automation and discourages us from thinking like aviators."

(Anonymous Pilot)

WHEN I BEGAN flying commercially in 1987 pilots attended a classroom to learn systems with a group of pilots and a subject matter expert. Today pilots learn systems on their own. In those early days a subject matter expert assessed the pilot's level of knowledge. This assessment method determined if the pilot had adequate understanding to proceed to the simulator. Pilots rarely know everything, and confusion often occurs when learning something new. Therefore the subject matter expert held a dual role—to asses adequate knowledge, and then to correct misunderstanding with an explanation. If the pilots' lack of understanding was unacceptable, then they would return to training.

Today, pilots take an electronic test, and if they achieve equal to or greater than an established percentage, they will pass. However, the lack of understanding on the missed responses may never be corrected. In addition, pilots have the opportunity to guess, versus leaving an answer blank, and could answer correctly simply because they got lucky. That process will leave a lack of understanding that does not get remedied. As it turns out, Atlas pilots take a traditional oral but may be transitioning toward an electronic assessment, which could create more of a problem with the level of understanding.

After the dissertation was complete, I looked into the Atlas crash by reaching out to Atlas pilots to learn what was happening in their training program. I wanted to know how a doctoral student statistically proved that their pilots lacked understanding, which was known to cause accidents and incidents, and yet eight years later a plane crashed for that very reason. *Did Atlas make an effort to fix their training?* What I learned was fascinating, but explained so much when a captain stated:

> *"We still do orals. Most of our evaluators use the oral as an opportunity to teach an understanding of a particular systems. The best evaluators anyway. Our problem is that the training, while long, has a fundamental flaw. It is written for the 10,000 hour jet pilot from bankrupt carriers such as Pan Am and Eastern. So these Millennials whose biggest body of water they ever flew over was lake Michigan are not being trained and don't have the experience. They can finish OE without ever seeing a NAT crossing. Had captains who couldn't take a rest because neither first officer knew what to do."*
>
> *Anonymous Pilot*

A preponderance of research and accident investigations attributed automation-related pilot errors, in part, to inadequate training. *Sub-optimal training* has been identified as one of the two most significant flight hazards, with the other being a shortage of experienced personnel.[21] Without experienced personnel, training becomes more essential. Without adequate training and experienced pilots, this becomes the single greatest flight hazard. Shortening training programs while pilots train themselves at home as cost saving measures have become an industry norm, and one in which the FAA has approved. A reduction in automation and flight management system (FMS) training has also become an FAA approved norm.[273]

> *"I am recently retired B767 Captain. After 30 year career I have observed hand flying skills deteriorate quite a bit with my first officers. However, they do an excellent job with the automation. Management doesn't have the time and money to cram in anything but the bare requirements for training session. [Airline] is good example, plus all the YouTube videos of pilots trying to land airplanes during windy conditions."*
>
> *(Anonymous Pilot)*

Airlines created standard operating procedures (SOP) where all pilots would perform the same processes and procedures in the flight deck. Safety is a crew event, not two pilots operating in isolation; yet, numerous accidents have been attributed, in part, to individual pilots not following SOPs. While one researcher attributed the lack of following SOPs to be a choice, *why* pilots ignored SOPs is a question of whether it was a pilot's conscious choice or a result of a cognitive overload due to training inadequacies, or simply lack of knowledge.[103]

Training and flight experience affect cognitive abilities, which further impact situation awareness. How pilots are trained will also impact learning capacity. Reducing factors that induce overload and restructuring information in a way that will enable pilots to formulate thoughts and assimilate previous knowledge, could improve learning and performance. The problem begins when training program managers don't understand how overload impacts the memory in their design of the simulator sessions. When the training session is filled with a large number of check-the-box requirements and time is limited due to a shortened footprint, this becomes a firehose approach to training and no learning is accomplished. Of the accidents reviewed by the Working Group over 30% were due to non-automation training, 23% were due to automation training, 15% was due to inadequate basic training, and 5% identified that automation was over-emphasized during evaluations.

> *"Automation really is changing how we do things and how we are taught to do things in new airplanes. Unfortunately, I feel that the school houses aren't doing a very good job. Been getting a lot of, "The manufacturer wanted us to tell you this, but we can't explain why or how." Last two initials I went through, I barely felt like I understood anything about how the aircraft functions systems wise."*
>
> *(Anonymous Pilot)*

Mode awareness issues have become the byproduct of automation, and the confusion in understanding automation functionality has been said to be due to lack of a mental representation of how the systems operated.[132] Training programs do not necessarily teach the pilot how the system operates. The pilot has the ability to memorize facts to pass training without assessment of actual understanding. The question of how much a pilot needs to know is a fair question with automated aircraft. The industry has shifted from an oral that included diagraming the electrical system of a B727, to an electronic test assessing memorized facts. While pilots do not need to be engineers, they must have a working understanding of the aircraft systems. If the aircraft is uncontrollably pitching forward, a pilot should know to disengage the stabilizer to stop that motion. However, pilots can only know what they know. If pilots are not trained because airlines and manufacturers have agreed to eliminate the requirement of a type-rating for new equipment, and regulators looks the other way, then how can we blame the pilot?

Automation complexity has increased the necessity of much needed training to master the automation, however, financial resources have yet to fulfill the requirement.[241] The OIG reported that the FAA is lacking in many areas of training mandates.[189] Unfortunately, there are no processes in place to confirm airline pilots received automation and monitoring training, to monitor how often the pilots manually fly, to judge whether they are proficient at manual flight, or to assess monitoring skills. As of 2019, the FAA has, however, mandated upset recovery training, manually flown arrival and departures, slow flight, loss of reliable airspeed, and recovery from stall and bounced landing training.

Beyond manually flown departures and arrivals, the focus of this pilot training mandate has shifted training from ensuring proficiency with primary flight skills and performance, to acceptance that flight control errors may occur when the automation fails or the pilot pushes the wrong button. Thus, the industry is focused on training the pilot *how to* recover once the abnormal condition manifests. Modern day automated aircraft are designed with protections to avoid unusual flight characteristics such as stalls, overbanking, and excessive speed. Yet if automation fails and the pilot has no flight skills to fall back on, the pilot may put the aircraft into an unusual condition that necessitates this type of trained escape maneuver. However, retention of this training may be in question if this is a one-time event during initial aircraft training, and the pilot may not experience such event until the end of their career. Cognitive performance requires practice and repetition for the pilot to remain proficient, and one-time events do not ensure proficiency. One might question if annual training would be enough.

> "I take it to heart being part of the generation of flying with no autopilot, here in Asia it's an exponential on-growing trend of over relying on automation, as if flying manual is dangerous, but of course to the industry is easy and cost beneficial to teach how to press buttons than to develop aviating skills. A real shame."
>
> (Anonymous Pilot)

Pilot training has shifted from a pilot-centered focus to a crew-based focus, yet the concept of learning has not been highlighted in this industry change. Learning, in part, is dependent upon cognition, repetition, assessment, and feedback. A critical view into pilot training may provide better understanding as to pilot deficiencies with mode awareness and operational programming errors.

16. Advanced Qualification Program (AQP)

"I have noticed a trend with new pilots. Their training is extremely basic and although they know the procedures well, they can't manually fly and do not understand the systems. I spend a lot of time teaching them how to land. They cannot even do it properly.

"Thanks to the reliability of the modern planes their lack of knowledge and skills is not obvious but will certainly come into consideration in degraded situations. Some of these young pilots are becoming captains and unfortunately will become the last fence in case of problem or unusual situation. I am not sure they have the resources to cope with that. I expect an increase in aviation accidents and incidents in the future due to this lack of skills."

(Anonymous Pilot)

Advanced Qualification Program (AQP) is a methodology used by many airlines to train pilots today. AQP is a 'train to proficiency' program that mandates inclusion of crew resource management (CRM), Line oriented flight training

(LOFT), and line operational evaluation (LOE) scenarios. While each airline can design their own program, AQP has mandatory requirements that must be followed:

- ✈ the simulator must be aircraft specific
- ✈ include indoctrination, qualification, and continuing qualification (CQ) programs
- ✈ include training and evaluation for instructors and examiners
- ✈ replicate normal flight operations
- ✈ include a normal crew complement
- ✈ collect proficiency data
- ✈ utilize a full flight simulator[86]

Under AQP, pilot training shifted from individual training and performance assessment to crew-based performance training. This line-oriented training process enables crews to manage the aircraft while improving team and communication skills. They are trained and tested as a crew. What we have seen however, is that understanding is a far greater concern as a causal factor of aircraft accidents, incidents, and pilot reports versus communication.

AQP is a voluntary program, yet when implemented is expected to exceed minimum training standards and demands. Concerns regarding this proficiency concept, that training would only be proficiency-based and focused on training efficiency—not on improved understanding and performance—at the expense of skill decline.[123] Yet, airlines have realized an economic benefit by reducing pilot training with AQP.

"We seem to do type ratings in the minimum time to save costs and it's effectively a box ticking exercise. We are the same re autothrottle or autothrust. Not to be ever taken out but we can dispatch with it u/s. We never practice it but we have to demonstrate our ability to fly a single engine ILS and go around every three years."

(Anonymous Pilot)

———————

Current training practices have enabled airlines to cancel traditional ground-schools. No longer do pilots come together in a classroom environment with an instructor and fellow classmates to learn aircraft operating systems. Under AQP, airline flight operations management authorizes pilots to teach themselves aircraft systems and computer operations via at-home training programs. This training process assumes a pilot will acquire correct systems understanding, and that when an inflight emergency arises the pilot will have accurate knowledge to deal with it. However, if inflight information is not understood or the pilot experiences cognitive overload, the pilot may make decisions based upon heuristics, a mental shortcut. While heuristics are purported to provide positive outcomes, this process may not lead to the best decision.[252]

An accident such as Air France Flight 447 presents a case where the wrong decision—to pull the stick aft at altitude—did not create a positive outcome. Another concern with the at-home methodology is that beginners do not have the knowledge and ability to determine what information is important and what is not relative to a given situation. It has been argued that for self-directed learning to be effective it should *not be* an isolated event, but requires a team to include teachers, mentors, and peers.[148]

Yet, under many approved AQP programs, pilots are expected to teach themselves aircraft systems without an instructor to facilitate questions, and without peers or support personnel, which may leave pilots short on understanding.

> *"The pilots just cannot be given a manual and then be expected to memorize the contents in order to transfer the knowledge to a practical application. Without meaningful reasoning for the pilots to understand the concepts, procedures, or tasks, the pilots only obtain rote knowledge level abilities without knowing how to apply the training content."*
>
> *Captain Wise, Ph.D.*[267]

While I am unsure whether Air France is operating under AQP or not, the issue with the AF447 accident was due to a lack of understanding followed by an improper response to the malfunction, because the pilots were never warned of a known issue. Therefore, an AQP program would not have benefited the level of understanding for those pilots or improved the safety culture.

Atlas is not training under AQP, but is training under Appendix F where pilots are individually trained. However, Atlas is currently in the process of transitioning to AQP. During this process, the training department has created a list of questions to use for orals. It appears this list may be in preparation for the electronic test. Unfortunately, the problem identified by Captain Wise's research and the reason for their 2019 crash were due to a lack of understanding, which is not being addressed. Therefore, the shift Atlas is considering doesn't appear to be focused on improving the level of understanding, but only a cost cutting measure. Based upon the research, cost cutting is an industry problem.

Training Assessment

> *"I had to learn on my own and nobody to ask questions.*
> *We don't have real manuals anymore, but all are on a*
> *computer. Not sure if I really know what I know, but then*
> *it doesn't seem anyone cares anyway."*
>
> (Anonymous Pilot)

The FAA has data identifying lack of understanding to be contributory to accidents and incidents, yet adequate assessment measures have yet to be addressed. Ascertaining training effectiveness through data collection in addition to crewmember, instructor, and evaluator assessment is an AQP mandate and integral component of training.

The fundamental connection between training and assessment is a dual role in effective training. The relationship between training and assessment is the fundamental core of AQP. Under AQP it is not sufficient to simply train. It must be demonstrated that the training ensures proficiency, and this can only be accomplished with quality assessments that identify precisely what aspects of the training program are working and what are not. The question that should be asked is, *"Are electronic tests effective assessment measures?"*

Safety control systems are designed around processes to gather data in order to improve safety. The primary reason for a data acquisition is to establish a systematic quality control system ensuring the efficacy of pilot training and qualification processes that foster continual improvement. The AQP guide provides an outline for how training and assessment data should be utilized to include:

→ Provide assurances of proficiency levels.

→ Establish expectations and determine variations from those expectations.

✈ Assess instructional quality.

✈ Validate training assumptions.

✈ Analyze effectiveness of instructors and evaluators.

✈ Provide instructor and evaluator feedback.

✈ Refine the training and/or measurement process.

✈ Indicate where training changes are needed.

✈ Validate alternative training technologies.

✈ Provide common grounds for sharing of information between carriers.

✈ Provide a quantitative means for CRM assessment.[86]

"I answered combination [oral and electronic question on the survey] because I was self-taught using a flash drive and then went to classroom where they gave the foot stomper questions that would be on the test so we could pass. The second part wasn't teaching more giving the answers."

(Anonymous Pilot)

Despite data collection requirements and guidelines as how to collect good data, adequate measurement of training effectiveness has eluded the industry. Many instructors assume pilots conduct walk-around procedures during operations, therefore due to a high volume of briefing material the instructor may not give the required oral and select "pass" during the required data collection process.

When simulator sessions are overloaded, an instructor may decide to omit items such as "land and hold short" training because they assume the pilot will reject that clearance anyway, and they don't have time to squeeze it in. What if an instructor is distracted in the simulator during a checking event with text messages? As he deals with personal problems while the pilots are flying the programmed scenario, it becomes impossible for an accurate assessment. A pilot can memorize facts and guess on the electronic test and pass. That doesn't mean they know what to do. Simulator sessions are also subjective, and sometimes the instructor is distracted and not paying attention.

Many years ago, I observed a captain instructor fumbling with the simulator panel not looking at the pilots, saying, "Good job, Good job". This instructor was confused with the operation of the simulator. During a checking event when the captain was the pilot flying, an emergency occurred shortly after takeoff, and the captain threw his hands up and said, "You've got it!" I took control and glanced back at the instructor. His chair was pushed as far back as he could go, and he was texting. Pilots deserve better than this, as do the passengers flying on their aircraft.

Pilot performance as identified by accidents, incidents, and ASRS. These events may be a better indicator of training ineffectiveness than current AQP data collection during simulator training events and electronic reviews.

> *"In Canada, there is no "oral" as part of a proficiency check. Depending on the operator, there may be a few questions prior to the ride, but usually it's just discuss the profile and then get in the sim and go do it."*
>
> *(Anonymous Pilot)*

Training assessment has been an ongoing challenge but, until recently, little research existed on effective simulator training evaluation, even though an effective evaluation is required by AQP. Concern lead to investigation of airline pilot assessment methods and the results identified:

"Examiners did not perceive and process all relevant facts (attributes) of an event, which mediated how they rated the performance… There is therefore mounting evidence that in the flight examiners' workplace, assessment is based on categorization, which can be mathematically modeled using fuzzy logic."[215]

Accepted training assessments do not necessarily substantiate that learning has taken place in the form of understanding and retention, with the capability to transfer that knowledge to the aircraft. Quality pilot training is a proactive safety strategy, which is dependent upon policy, risk management, safety assurance, and safety promotion—all elements of a Safety Management System (SMS). The AQP guide was designed to assist training and assessment with safety assurance and safety promotion, the focus of SMS, where corporate culture may be the key to success—or as the results of this research identified, the core of the problem.

Nothing can replace a human for knowledge assessment.

Learning

> *"I had to google the cockpit of my plane because the
> company flash drive manual was in black n white and
> aircraft symbols mean different things depending on their
> color. Never have I seen training so bad in all my years of
> airline flying. Scary where the kids will be who don't have
> experience to fall back on to help understand systems and
> operations."*
>
> *(Anonymous Pilot)*

LEARNING OCCURS WHEN systems knowledge and procedures move from the working memory into the long-term memory. Information processing and knowledge acquisition are key aspects of learning, where competency defines knowledge application. In order to learn, pilots must not only have aptitude, but they must also have the ability to practice through repetition, receive feedback, and feel confident that the level of performance they achieve will ensure a safe operation.

Yet, there is a disparity between initial pilot training (where the pilot learns a new aircraft) and effective line operations (once on the flight line) when it comes to managing the automated aircraft. Training that lacks repetition and feedback in complex aircraft may directly impact understanding (knowledge), performance (manual flying), and pilot confidence in automated aircraft. It's been argued that pilots cannot learn skills with *only* explicit instruction and declarative knowledge acquisition. Furthermore, flight skills depend upon multiple environmental, physiological, and aircraft cues acquired through repetition.[168]

Adult learning research indicates that pilot experience, reflection upon that experience, real world application of training elements with problem centered training, and internal versus external motivation, improves learning.[44] Airline training processes, however, utilize a behavioristic approach, which opposes the construct of learner directed, adult learning concepts.[267] Pilot-centered training aligned with adult learning practices focuses on metacognitive concepts emphasizing self-evaluation and improves learning.

Many airlines also use computer-based training (CBT) to teach pilots aircraft systems. However, research indicates that CBT focuses on declarative knowledge only, versus how that knowledge will be applied to the operation, and contradicts adult learning theory. Problems with CBT design that have no foundation in adult learning principles included rote memorization of acronyms, and may leave pilots short on understanding.

Cognition

COGNITION IS THE mental process of acquiring knowledge and associated understanding through thought, experience, and all senses. Cognition is required for learning as well as sustained performance. Yet, when working memory is overloaded with too much complex, illogical information, data do not transfer to long-term memory, which prohibits memory formation. Cognitive Load Theory (CLT) suggests the reduction of causal factors causing overload and restructuring information in a manner where pilots are able to formulate thoughts associated with previous knowledge would improve information processing and memory formation.[139]

Automated glass cockpit and fly-by-wire aircraft are highly complex equipment, and training manuals present tremendous amounts of unfamiliar information. Simulator events that overload the pilots add to this challenge. The pilot is required to read, comprehend, transfer, and retain that information in long-term memory for practical application at a later date. Pilots are also expected to learn, retain, and transfer this knowledge from an at-home, train-yourself program, without support or clarification. The question must be asked how this process is okay, when confusion and lack of understanding have been identified as the causal factors of inadequate performance, resulting in accidents, incidents, and pilot safety reports.

Industry performance indicates that training methodologies are a problem. Yet, FAA mandates have not addressed current training processes, where the first stage of skill development is declarative knowledge acquisition. Nonetheless, declarative knowledge without associated understanding is likened to rote memorization leading to poor situation awareness. Success of training processes is dependent upon pilots' experience, closeness to the new information, perseverance, and the availability of resources.[64] This is where experience will help the success of learning.

> *The next generation of pilots will not enter the industry with experience and will not obtain that experience in current operations.*

Low-level learning impacts pilots' SA. In that when an unexpected event occurs and confusion disables the pilot from understanding the meaning of that experience, the pilot is unable to project the status into the future. This lack of understanding decreases decision-making ability impacting the safety of the flight.

Pilot Debrief and Feedback

THE GOAL OF a debrief is to learn where reflection on performance can impact operational safety. However, systematic reflection, where pilots analyze and evaluate behavior relating to performance, requires feedback on both the outcome—success or failure—and how to improve the process.[61]

The power of the flight crew debrief has been the focus of much research and is instrumental in how pilots learn from human error. Learning also depends upon how the debrief is conducted per the outcome of the event. If the checkride was a success, the debrief should only focus upon errors made throughout the event to maximize learning, yet after a failed experience the focus must also include what the pilot did correctly. The need to accurately assess the experience is necessary for learning to occur, and pilots become more accountable for their behavior if they become responsible for their successes and failures during the learning process.[61] The pilot debrief contains elements of both feedback and self-assessment.

"I had to select the option "less than 15 minutes", [regarding length of debrief] but the truth is we never had a debrief during my entire initial training. Granted it was late at night and the instructor wanted to get home, but training was a firehose event and by the next day I forgot what we did the night before. I really depend on debriefs so I can take notes and review for the next day and when I get to the line."

(Anonymous Pilot)

Feedback is an essential component of learning. During AQP required instructor training, the question must be asked whether instructors understand how feedback improves learning. Literature supporting pre- and post-briefs, indicates that effective feedback should be task-focused versus person-oriented. It should also include self-critiques that are participatory in nature, and where individuals are willing to accept feedback from others. Training that lacks repetition and feedback in complex aircraft may directly impact understanding (knowledge), performance (hand flying), and pilot confidence.

Cognitive skills must be utilized and practiced often, despite initial learning, to maintain competency. Not only are practice and repetition necessary components of competency, but are also essential to learning in creating automaticity and adaptive expertise. However, learning requires more than practice, it requires reflection upon that practice to improve performance.[170] The power of a video utilized during a pilot debrief with the flight instructor and seat support pilot are integral parts of the debrief, and appear to be missing in many cases. Learning is not an isolated event. A picture is worth a thousand words. When students observe their performance via video, and self-assessment and reflection are accomplished with an instructor and peers, maximum performance gains will be realized.

The length of a training session, in addition to the debrief, may also impact learning performance. Flight training simulator lessons have historically been conducted in four-hour sessions. However, the four-hour session has left the pilots fatigued and less apt to remember what happened during the training event, contrary to effective reflection. A researcher suggested a 3-hour session, as it was discovered that the pilots to be more amicable to discussing the training session in detail, due in part to less fatigue and more timely memory of events.[170] This indicates that shorter simulator sessions, with extended debrief, including videos, would support improved learning performance. Historically the four-hour session was utilized with individual based training titled Appendix F, where each pilot received two hours of training. However, today pilots are trained as a crew under AQP, and the three-hour session would be more effective under line-oriented training. This suggestion is not to eliminate those training hours, but to add additional training events to the current footprint. The quality of training would greatly improve.

The pilot debrief also provides an opportunity for feedback which has been linked to improved performance. It has been suggested that the benefits of feedback in aviation training have been the most undervalued benefit, denying the pilot an opportunity for self-assessment.[24]

Self-Assessment

AVIATION SAFETY IS judged by the lack of accidents. This assumption could be equally as flawed as the teenager who has been running red traffic lights for years and believes that his behavior is safe because he hasn't had an accident. Pilots may view their personal performance based upon safely landing at destination versus whether or not boundaries of safety were breached. Pilots also lack means to assess their knowledge or level of performance in order to improve during daily operations.

Automated aircraft provide extensive latitude for safety, meaning there is a great deal of room for error. Automation is a safety net that minimizes consequences of pilot performance. Therefore, pilots may perform and respond to mismanaged arrivals, poor decision-making, and lack of SA without resulting in a consequential event. Continued success may then create erroneous mental models of adequate performance.[57]

> "Fatigue and company pressure is also an extremely important part of the risk factor. I have also noticed a trend with new pilots. Their training is extremely basic and although they know the procedures well they can't manually fly and do not understand the systems. I spend a lot of time teaching them how to land. They cannot even do it properly.
>
> "Thanks to the reliability of the modern planes their lack of knowledge and skills is not obvious but will certainly come into consideration in degraded situations. Some of these young pilots are becoming captains and unfortunately will become the last fence in case of problem or unusual situation. I am not sure they have the resources to cope with that. I expect an increase in aviation accidents and incidents in the future due to this lack of skills."
>
> (Anonymous Pilot)

While self-assessment is an integral part of effective learning, pilots must possess the resources to accurately measure performance in order to adjust their self-assessments. Assessments should not only provide continuous feedback that identifies individual progress and areas for improvement but should also be based upon an established level of performance, with self-assessment an essential component.

FOQA data is gathered and utilized by airlines to identify operational performance, yet the pilot is never made aware of that performance unless the level of performance has crossed a line into a hazard potential. Performance data, if provided to the pilots, could be used to assess their daily performance in order to improve. Self-assessment extends to assessing performance in daily operations. Under AQP, the training itself should also be assessed. The financial expense to enable a pilot to access their personal performance would be negligible, and the results could prevent the next accident.

17. Safety Culture and SMS

"Look into the corporate culture, run by non-aviation personnel with better perks, which has bull dozed the airlines in the few couple of decades. Pilots are treated like bus drivers now."

(Anonymous Pilot)

A CORPORATION'S MISSION statement does not necessarily identify a company's culture. While airlines declare their values on paper, if the behavior is contradictory to those value statements, the behavior identifies the corporate culture. That old saying actions speak louder than words works well with culture identification. Corporate culture is the shared behavior and values—stemming from artifacts, espoused values and beliefs, underlying assumptions, policies and procedures, and safety culture—that characterize an organization's nature.[222, 240] The Federal Aviation Administration (FAA) defines safety culture as, "the shared values, actions, and behaviors that demonstrate a commitment to safety over competing goals and demands," and comprises five subcultures— reporting culture, just culture, flexible culture, informed culture, and learning culture.[77] Results identified a negative safety culture worldwide, which is negatively impacting pilot training and resulting performance.

> *"I myself had been that "operator-pilot" when I used to fly in Russia where hand flying is strongly discouraged and the punitive culture of low uncertainty tolerance prevails. Joining [Airline] was a transformative experience when I realized that manual flying is still a thing."*
>
> *(Anonymous Pilot)*

> *"One day, you should investigate the reporting culture in China. Their punishment culture."*
>
> *(Anonymous Pilot)*

Policies are a company's written rules. However, a company's written policy does not necessarily define expected behavior. When the company writes "do this" but enforces different behavior, the *unwritten* rules become an element of a negative safety culture.

> *"Many pilots like to fly manually and manual flight is requested in all simulator training in China. The problem is the punishment culture for any deviation based in QAR data. So it's better to keep all automation engaged in order to reduce the risk of flight deviations."*
>
> *(Anonymous Pilot)*

"Where discussing auto flight v. Manual flight your survey touches on corporate requirements/policy. My airline for example has conflicting policies on this. It states in part of our FCOM that we are to use automation as much as possible, later on in the same manual and in the SOP it states that pilots will maintain hand flying skills. It does not give guidelines as to when or how this is to be accomplished."

(Anonymous Pilot)

"I recently finished a captain checkout on the B777 with 25-yrs previous flying Captain on the 74. During training the instructors said to never disengage the autothrust. But the then [Airline] put out a training video recommending that the pilots should disengage the autothrust and the importance of doing so, telling pilots to memorize power settings in order to fly etc. (In my opinion wrong… a pilot needs to know how to manage the aircraft.) During line ops I was told that we never disengage the autothrust on this aircraft. The company manuals and training state one thing for FAA approval, but the company doesn't follow their own rules. That's how they roll. I think the FAA knows and doesn't care. The fox is guarding the henhouse sort of thing."

(Anonymous Pilot)

Safety culture is the essence of the corporation's culture—behaviors, values, beliefs, and how the organization does business relative to safety and associated processes. That includes communication, reporting, flexibility, information sharing, and improvement strategies. Therefore, safety culture defines corporate culture. Unfortunately, the culture of many airlines are not indicative of a safety culture.

"A few of my colleagues at that time told me while they were CFIs in China some of the students would taxi out, set the parking brake, hop out and have a smoke and let the HOBBS meter spin never doing ANY of their solo flying. The management encouraged this as it kept the tach times low (!!!!!!!!). This was from multiple sources at different schools. Imagine seeing 2-3 planes in a run-up with props spinning and NOBODY in them."

(Anonymous Pilot)

———————

Safety culture emphasizes communication in a flexible, blame-free, accountable environment that encourages reporting safety concerns. An environment where management has both the knowledge and ability to support the system's overall safety goals focused on continual improvement. An airline's safety culture establishes the foundational support of a successful safety management system (SMS). SMS is defined as:

> *"An organization-wide comprehensive and preventive approach to managing safety. An SMS includes a safety policy, formal methods for identifying hazards and mitigating risk, and promotion of a positive safety culture. An SMS also provides assurance of the overall safety performance of your organization."* [81]

SMS risk mitigation and safety assurance are designed to improve overall organizational performance in preparation for NextGen. Thus, the FAA mandated all U.S. airlines to have an SMS in effect as of January 2018. SMS importance extends beyond regulatory compliance, but also makes logical business sense in comparison to the costs associated with an accident. However, in order to be effective, SMS demands a positive safety culture—reporting culture, just culture, flexible culture, informed culture, and learning culture.[240] SMS implementation will be in name only without a positive safety culture. An SMS that is in name only is not only ineffective, but the airline is also in violation of federal standards. It remains questionable, however, whether or not the FAA regulators overseeing these airlines have an understanding of SMS requirements. Lack of regulatory enforcement could simply be attributed to lack of knowledge of their own regulations versus lack of oversight. Regardless, the results are the same.

> *"There were some questions which didn't give me the choice of saying that I am doing certain things because the company SOP requires it. For example, we are not allowed to fly manually by many airlines. Also, the fear culture in some Airlines. That means managements behavior towards pilots.*
>
> *"Mostly pilots in major airlines do things or don't do things because they don't want to get in trouble with the management n called into the office. I have worked for six airlines and the reason of leaving was to go to an airline who respects their pilots. Most of them harass pilots through the flight data monitoring system. Some airlines have negative training through instructors who overload you with multiple failures n shouting n degrading in the PCs. Some make u feel absolutely inadequate through the company's culture n SOPs. I can go on forever."*
>
> *(Anonymous Pilot)*

Corporate culture also plays a key role in pilots' performance beyond espoused values, corporate rules, and written procedures, in that the unwritten rules are what often guide behavior and impact performance. Corporate culture therefore extends to performance in that *how* the airline culture behaves transcends employee performance standards.

If the informal, unwritten motto of the people in an organization is "the best way to advance in this organization is to shut up and not make waves", the entire professional force will eventually lower their personal performance standards.[24] Unfortunately, this what the majority of pilots surveyed believe to be the case.

> *"Deviation from standard operating practices (normalization of deviance) may become the normal practice when the organization encourages, or pushes operating limits."*
>
> Robert Besco

Just as SMS demands safety assurance, maximizing safety efforts requires performance monitoring and improvement measures, feedback, and recognition of positive performance to ensure operational efficiency with maximized safety efforts. The importance of a learning organization is that it encourages employees to improve their knowledge, to experiment and try novel methods of problem solving and to search out feedback.[105] Unfortunately, many airlines, at best, meet regulatory requirements, but compliance does not necessarily mean to the highest standards.[21] The practice of only meeting minimal regulatory compliance diminishes hazard identification and risk mitigation processes required for SMS.

The evolution of airline safety includes hazard identification and risk mitigation, supported by an informed and learning culture. Human factors research drove the creation of CRM, AQP, threat and error management (TEM), and LOSA in an attempt to reduce pilot error and improve safety. Crew resource management (CRM), originally termed cockpit resource management, became the first regulatory mandate to teach crewmembers interpersonal and communication skills in order to reduce pilot error.

CRM was not a one-time fix, but an evolutionary process during the 1990s that encompassed five stages expanding over a decade—theory, teamwork emphasis, team expansion, AQP, and threat and error management (TEM). AQP required CRM training in the form of LOFT and LOE scenarios. This shift in training moved from an individual-based performance focus to a crew-based focus to improve communication. TEM was designed to assist pilots in identifying operational threats in order to mitigate risk. The understanding was that errors would occur. However, if pilots' awareness expanded to potential threats, pilots would then become prepared for those events that would otherwise have been unexpected.

LOSA created the platform for trained observers to monitor performance on actual flights, document threats, and record scores based upon pre-established behavior criteria. However, multiple issues have created a concern with the efficacy of LOSA:

→ lack of feedback for improvement
→ inability to identify the entire chain of event
→ inability to assess pilots' understanding of the aircraft and operations
→ how TEM was connected to the LOSA process to mitigate risk

✈ failure of data to improve operational processes[157]

The aviation industry is moving to more proactive safety measures, somewhat likened to TEM with risk mitigation, but extended beyond the flight deck to the entire corporation. SMS demands entire organizational processes to proactively look at operational practices, identify threats, and mitigate risk. Communication is essential. SMS should become an integral part of every organization's safety culture, not only to comply with FAA mandates, but for improved organizational safety. However, unless leadership understands SMS, the effectiveness will be non-existent. It's become apparent during my research that SMS is one of the most least understood FAA regulations. Which makes one wonder if this regulation is nothing but a piecrust regulation—easily made and easily broken.

> *"Cabin crew from far eastern countries (South Korea, China, Japan) will never contradict you or let you know if you are wrong, NEVER! (quite a big threat!) They tend to speak English not fluently and will never ask you to explain again what you just said and they did not understand. Their authority gradient is HUGE in their countries."*
>
> (Anonymous Pilot)

The Continental Express Flight 2574 and ValueJet Flight 592 accidents were attributed to corporate culture and began the shift to an aviation organizational safety culture.[181, 182] A culture in which management attitudes, beliefs, actions, norms, rules, and acceptable levels of risk moved to the forefront. The above accidents were identified to be a corporate issue, in that

Safety culture is the enduring value and priority placed on worker and public safety by everyone in every group at every level of an organization. It refers to the extent to which individuals and groups will commit to personal responsibility for safety, act to preserve, enhance and communicate safety concerns, strive to actively learn, adapt and modify (both individual and organizational) behavior based on lessons learned from mistakes, and be rewarded in a manner consistent with these values.[265]

To exemplify a safety culture attitude, a CEO at a major airline stated,

"Every employee has the right and authority on an unfettered basis to stop the operation at any time. Every single employee has the right, the responsibility, and the duty to stop the operation if anything is not right in the operation."

This CEO further stated,

"We're going to comply with the regulations; that's absolutely the goal… And then we all culturally have to figure out how to encourage the open, transparent safety reporting throughout our organizations."

Despite this CEO's assertion of a reporting culture, fifteen Air 21 whistle blower actions (Wendell H. Ford Aviation Investment and Reform Act for the 21st Century) have been filed against this airline, due to retaliation against employees reporting safety violations from 2008 to 2018, and forty-two court cases of harassment have been recorded (FOIA, 2018).

An effective SMS also requires the organizational safety culture to facilitate line employees' ability to implement SMS principles in daily operational duties while the organization assesses performance. I'm in agreement with the researchers who believe a gap may exist between employee involvement, corporate assessment, and proactive response.[36] As identified, a huge gap exists when employees are afraid to bring information forward.

American Airlines Flight 587, an Airbus A330 crashed in 2001 due to incorrect rudder response during a wake turbulence encounter presents an example of this gap. The aircraft became unstable and began to roll due to wake vortices of an aircraft that had just departed ahead of it. Despite the pilot flying being advised by experienced pilots, that he should not be slamming his foot into the rudder pedal, this pilot was performing in the manner he had been trained. This crash was attributed to incorrect procedures, however, numerous documents surfaced years after the crash that identified an incorrect process in upset recovery training had been a known training issue that many people had attempted to address to no avail.[93] The comment from many instructors was (and is often heard today) "It works in the simulator". Yet, due to lack of communication and information sharing, required with informed, reporting and learning cultures, essential to a safety culture, this information was never addressed until *after* the accident and 260 people died.

Unfortunately, the lack of information sharing lessons with the American crash went unheeded. The AF447 crash should never have occurred, either. In what has remained hidden from the public is that numerous pilot static system faults had previously occurred, yet because those events did not result in a crash nothing was done. The pilots wrote ASAP reports, therefore the FAA knew. The airline(s) knew of the incident, but did not warn the pilots or create the necessary training. Not until AF447 crashed, and 270 people died, did effective change take place by fixing the component that was faulty and implement training. The Senate Commerce Committee learned of these events and yet that information did not impact the majority's decision-making for the future of aviation safety.

> *"I'm an old pilot from GA and the B727, DC9-80, MD80 ,B767 A320/330/340 with approximately. 25K hours on everything. What really worries me, is that you are encouraged NOT to fly manually, not to fly visual and that we are getting punished in China if doing so... I got punished with 1500 USD, for continuing under VMC conditions, (CAVOK), down to 500 feet AGL. Stabilized at 550 feet as required by Boeing and Airbus, but punished as they do not allow us to fly VMC approaches as stated by FAA and EASA. And I took over and flew it manually. Big mistake. These guys will never, never be able to cope with an unusual situation, that requires manual flying. And most of these guys do NOT, understand English beyond the very basics as required in an emergency situation. Maybe FAA and EASA should introduce English requirements to foreign pilots (Chinese) as the Chinese are doing towards US."*
>
> (Anonymous Pilot)

*"Until very recently our airline used the training depart-
ment (with very specific instructors) as a punitive medium,
or cost control medium (I have been affected by both),
so more detail into how the ACTUAL company culture
affects the safe operation and or learning environment
could be explored."*

(Anonymous Pilot)

While the FAA continues an attempt to balance safety and economics, economics appears to be winning. Early technology was improved upon to reduce systems failure and adapt human factors into design. Human error resulting in communication problems prompted the safety side of the FAA to create CRM, while the economics side developed AQP. Under AQP, the combination of communication training was incorporated into the LOFT and LOE scenarios to improve performance. While at the same time it enabled airlines to decrease the amount of training to save money. Subsequently a new generation of automated accidents occurred due to lack of understanding, confusion, mode awareness, and flight skill loss.

Economics are driving NextGen, and the FAA is working toward safer skies during this change with proactive measures via safety culture and SMS mandates. However, if operators do not have a safety culture to support SMS, this effort will be for nothing. If FAA regulators overseeing these airlines lack knowledge, then unsafe practices will continue. Accidents, incidents, and ASRS continue due to lack of understanding, confusion, mode awareness, and flight skill loss, all of which are training issues. Safety culture is the foundation of SMS, which will facilitate a safer environment for NextGen operations. However, a gap appears to exist between safety culture, SMS, NextGen, and training, resulting in ongoing performance issues.

Experts predict an increase in the accident rate
to an unacceptable level from 2020-2025, due
to added complexity of air-based systems.[197]

With the added complexity of the NextGen environment, human error in automated aircraft is likely to increase if pilots are not properly trained to achieve deeper understanding of aircraft operations. While corporate culture impacts performance in multiple ways, an unethical culture negatively impacts the safe operation and will not support an SMS.

Worldwide Company Policy

I WAS ASKED, "How do you know these are unwritten policies and not just how they do things?" My answer was—does it matter? How we do things and unofficial mandates are both part of the culture. Despite the semantics of unwritten policy or we call it just the way we do things because that's what were told to do. This is part of culture. The following pilot comments identify an element of safety culture, as policy and operational practice. The fascinating aspect is when you read these comments, you'll understand what's happening in the real world of commercial aviation regarding company policy and automation.

"As per the company, any & all "Raw-Data" flying is sup-
posed to be done during the simulator sessions. Airbus as a
manufacturer in a way also prefers that it be flown using
all the automation available… but that is not to detract
from the fact that if something ain't right, you take over!
One of the 'Airbus Golden Rules'!"

(Anonymous Pilot)

"My operator's policy is that the autopilot may be disengaged as the pilot wishes, however the auto thrust should remain engaged until 50'AGL at the latest. It was difficult for me to answer your Qs accurately given that. In Canada, 2 pilots can operate long legs (7-10hrs) without a third pilot. Usually it is a pilot agreement mandated requirement for augmented crews unless the flight is ultra long haul. There is an amendment of the regs in the works, but it is taking excruciatingly long to implement."

(Anonymous Pilot)

"We are restricted from disconnecting AT during all phases of Flight unless dictated by the QRH during non-normal situations. We are also required to engage auto Flight during RNAV SIDs that require accurate lateral naviga-tion, especially in Europe. There was no restrictions on the 737 and 767 and for that matter the 777 (autothrottles were recommended) The 787 sop's require AT always and Auto pilot recommendations."

(Anonymous Pilot)

"I worked at [Airline] before, which has one of the strictest policies regarding manual flight. Raw data (flight directors off) was banned as of last year, and manual flight is banned in most busy airports, as the "airport briefings" the company publishes state "Mandatory use of AP". Manual flight is also banned from most smaller airports, again the "airport briefings" state "Mandatory use of AP due to possible VFR traffic". Which leaves very little room for hand-flying the aircraft legally. I would say less than 5% of [Airline] pilots would regularly or even occasionally hand-fly the aircraft above 1000 ft."

(Anonymous Pilot)

"Our company policy is AP can be disconnected below 10000 ft, but FD and AT shall be ON except in case of non-normal or MELs. So it is "Highly unlikely" I will disconnect AP and AT for the arrival or the approach as it is a company policy, but I would like to do it!"

(Anonymous Pilot)

"I am passionate on the subject, I was a Mariner sailing on Cargo ships for 20 years the switched careers to a flying job, I will forward to other pilots I know and have completed the survey myself. W.r.t to the automation questions I did my initial training on the A320 with a smaller airline with a number of older trainers from purely civil as defense back grounds who encouraged manual flight—however I am now a check pilot myself and company policies with my current employer do not permit manual flying above 1000 feet on routine line flights and permit on Auto pilot or Auto thrust disconnection not both at the same time. Most new pilots therefore and not habitual to include air speed in their scan."

(Anonymous Pilot)

"I've completed your survey. It is an interesting topic to me because I have been flying at 2 different airlines where the former required as much automation as possible and the latter required the PROPER automation for the situation, where manual flight without AP/AT and FD is highly encouraged and flown like this I would say on every 5th leg."

(Anonymous Pilot)

"Our policy about flying with AP/AT is written in our OMA. It is recommended to use AP/AT as it lowers the workload, however we are allowed to fly manual for practice. It is not recommended in the TMA, but in the final stage I encourage it as much as practicable."

(Anonymous Pilot)

"My company prefers to use automation to the extreme, and they do the training to the extreme usage of SOP! NO manual FLIGHT! I was lucky to fly manually years ago when there was no EICAS/EFIS."

(Anonymous Pilot)

"Our ops manual requires the highest level of automation at all times so we are not allowed to turn off the autothrust and/or flight directors at any time. We are however, allowed to hand fly the airplane below 10,000 ft. I personally try to do that as much as possible, but I have flown with numerous pilots who turn on the autopilot as soon as the gear is up and disconnect only around 400-500 ft on final."

(Anonymous Pilot)

"I fly the 737 in a company where manual flying is accepted but I can see the tendency of forcing pilots to be less and less "pilots" of the airframe more than vectors of accomplishing the daily duty quite obvious. I hear some companies in Europe now force pilot to use LNAV/VNAV for visual approach as mandatory, or Asiatic companies even force the use of AP and AT down to minimum or the aircraft manual minimum, which I find compelling."

(Anonymous Pilot)

"My current airline inherits a much more pragmatic Schandinavian culture, has more relaxed SOP's and strongly encourages manual flight, including raw data hand-flying. Around 90% of my colleagues hand-fly the departure to around 10,000 feet and disconnect on base leg during the approach. About 20 to 30% of hand-flown departures and approaches are flown with Flight Directors off."

(Anonymous Pilot)

"The aircraft I fly (Airbus A320 Family) or the Company's automation policy prevents me from disconnecting every-thing on routine flights. AutoThrust remains the engaged in all phases of flight from thrust reduction altitude till the flare, when the thrust levers are retarded for all normal flights. The only exception being in case of a failure."

(Anonymous Pilot)

"My present company mandates the use of ALL auto-mation from 10000ft-10000ft. Below that ONLY the Autopilot may be disengaged, but FDs & A/THR need to be engaged. My previous company which got me my initial experience on the A320, did however have flexi-bility in these areas & I was lucky enough to benefit from flying without AP/FD & A/THR on regular line flights occasionally to practice & keep my skills sharp. The present day scenario however has scores of pilots from varying backgrounds & experience and it is therefore no wonder the company mandates the use of automation."

(Anonymous Pilot)

"When asked about written company policies "requiring" automation, I answered "yes". To be more specific, our company has a written policy requiring the use of automation during RNAV departures, but encourages "hand-flying" when conditions permit, so there was no absolutely correct answer. My personal thought about the use of "partial" automation is as follows; during a hand flown approach, autothrottles should be disconnected when the autopilot is disconnected. The reason I feel this way is that any pitch change made by the pilot during the approach causes a change in airspeed. Autothrottles will respond in order to maintain the selected speed. As the throttles move, the pilot will then need to re-adjust his pitch, which will cause a corresponding change with the thrust setting, which will then require... You can see the cycle that begins to happen."

(Anonymous Pilot)

"Highest available level was consciously worded like this, meaning not to exclude any approach or airport option due to a technical issue. You can still fly non-precision-approaches in IMC with ATHR defect, because you are still highest available.

"From experience, this policy gives plenty of opportunity to practice manual skills, while making a clear statement under which circumstances highest support of automation must be used."

(Anonymous Pilot)

"Just two sentences define all you need: 1. manual flight (with or without FD) equals manual thrust 2. Non-ILS approaches are flown at the highest available level of automation until Rwy is in sight and identified. I feel this policy [combined with the principle that manual flight (with or without FD) also means manual thrust] is the clearest, most sensible and most practical way of a sensible usage of automation while keeping crews skilled AND comfortable in manual flight. It should be adopted by more airlines in my opinion."

(Anonymous Pilot)

———————

"We can hand fly the jet at sensible times but not without the auto throttle."

(Anonymous Pilot)

———————

"I hear and read that many Companies in the World require and mandate full automation during the whole flight… what I think of it is that it is contraproductive to safety! I agree that the autopilot flies better than a human but it flies only what the human tells it to fly! I am very lucky that I still fly and work in the Company that doesn't forbid manual flying… should any problem occur to a pilot who flies only with automation, she/he in that crucial moment doesn't have necessary confidence to do and to finish the things routinely with her/his own hands! That's tha fact!!! I know since I have seen the things! Manual flying should be encouraged in certain percentage in 30 days or so!"

(Anonymous Pilot)

———————

"I found some questions I couldn't really answer the way I should. For example, about automation my actual company discourages to disengage but for me is not a problem because on the contrary in the previous company when proper conditions the company could encourage to disconnect. But honestly the local pilots of my actual company are mostly really bad pilots so I understand. In my last simulator the captain was not even able to land twice flying a circling approach."

(Anonymous Pilot)

———————

"We have a policy when to go fully automated, it goes like this: "Non-ILS approaches are flown at the highest available level of automation until Rwy is in sight and identified."

(Anonymous Pilot)

———————

"In VMC conditions, with the runway in sight, independent of the type of approach, you can fly how you want (if allowed by airspace design, STAR design etc.): automatics on, automatics off, with or without FD if you choose automatics off (however AP off always means also ATHR off, these two are linked together). At the end, we are pilots, and we can steer an aircraft manually into the touchdown zone within speed, bank, pitch and VS limits. The same applies to ILS approaches: you choose what you use (except in LowVis Ops, there clear rules apply)."

(Anonymous Pilot)

———————

"However, in all other approaches, without the runway in sight, we use highest avail level of automation: that means AP, ATHR and FD, but also highest FMA-modes of the autoflight system. The reason is: IMC non-precision-approaches are far more demanding than ILS-approaches or approaches in VMC, so we want full mental capacity, therefore highest available level of automation."

(Anonymous Pilot)

18. Aviation Passion

"I do take great pride in being a pilot, but it does not define me."

(Anonymous Pilot)

I WONDERED—*WOULD PILOT performance vary with the level of passion?* Someone with passion for an activity would obviously give more effort because of their love for that activity. However, would that include manual flight? Could it overcome other factors that may be impacting manual flight? If passion did impact performance for the positive, could it affect the future of pilot hiring?

There was a time when pilots exhibited passion for flying during the employment interview. That passion reignited the passion of the management pilot interviewing them, who subsequently said, "you're hired." There was a time when all pilots loved flying, and the love of aviation handshake opened doors. Unfortunately, pilot hiring has shifted to a check the box mentality where non-pilot managers are often included as pilot hiring decision makers. If the industry had a better understanding of how passion impacted performance, pilot hiring methodologies could adjust for that passionate pilot. Therefore, research into defining passion and understanding how it affects pilots was needed.

Passion has been associated with an individual's strong involvement in a favorite activity and defined as, "a strong inclination toward an activity that people like, find important and which they invest their time and energy."[249] When passion is focused on aviation that individual is termed an AvGeek. An AvGeek is defined as "someone who is passionate about aviation and that passion can be shown in countless ways," including photography, aviation club participation, reading aviation magazines and books, flying home simulators, or owning aircraft models.[27] An AvGeek does not necessarily have to be a pilot, but if the pilot were to be an AvGeek, their passion toward aviation could be carried into the job with a potential for increased performance.

> *"I still enjoy hand flying when I can regardless of having 26,000 + hours."*
>
> *(Anonymous Pilot)*

Passion is not one size fits all. Two types of passion exist: harmonious passion and obsessive passion. Harmonious passion is the essence of an AvGeek, where the passion is internalized into the pilot's identity, the individual is highly motivated and dedicated, and the passion is in harmony with their life. A harmonious activity will be fulfilling, gratifying, and fun-filled where the passionate person experiences enjoyment.[10] The differences between harmonious passion and work engagement is that the passionate person identifies with their passion, and work engagement represents the person's feeling toward work.[221] Work engagement has also been compared to job passion when personal identification and satisfaction with the job exist.[125] Aviation passion combined with the job of flying could create a harmonious passion that is both representative of job satisfaction and personal passion, creating increased work engagement.

People with harmonious passion have better work performance, However those with job passion feel more identification and satisfaction, enhancing their desire to perform well because there is a personal meaning and love for the job. When a pilot is passionate about aviation, in addition to enjoyment, the pilot's self-concept within that passion becomes their identity.

> *"I've found those that flew in Alaska in smaller airplanes, those that continue to fly small GA planes are more in tuned with the jet—the hand/eye coordination but this should come as no shocker. I've only met one jet pilot who owned a GA plane, a tail wheel nonetheless, and he was just a crappy pilot regarding landings. Go figure."*
>
> (Anonymous Pilot)

It's been said that harmonious passion exists because the individual loves the job characteristics, not because they have to do the work for social approval.[125] Obsessive passion, however, based upon identity, can lead to feelings of superiority and importance. Obsessive passion also stems from the need for social acceptance and self-esteem.[149] Meaning, the identity of what a pilot means becomes the driving force for the passion, more so than the enjoyment. Harmonious passion was identified to be a positive force on performance, as opposed to obsessive passion.

Elements of passion in regard to focus and immersion versus absorption, depend upon intentional concentration and the quality of effort. The pilot with greater harmonious passion should have greater absorption manifesting into higher levels of performance.

Attention, however, does not necessarily increase performance, attention could be due to job complexity, greater challenges, and higher demands, all which are associated with highly automated aircraft.

> *"It amazed me how incredibly uninhibited most of my captains of previous generation had been when it would come to downgrading automation levels to basic raw data flying when either a situation dictated that or purely for enjoyment of flying. Eventually, I am proud to say, I have become that pilot, too. Granted those were less automated airplanes (E145 and CRJ-700) than A320 that I had operated overseas, with no A/T and integrated vertical navigation."*
>
> *(Anonymous Pilot)*

Researchers identified that work engagement increased performance related to passion based on three dimensions.[221] First, the individual must be dedicated, resilient, with the ability to persevere despite problems. Second, they must be inspired, proud, enthusiastic, and realize the significance and challenges of their work. Third, they must be engrossed and absorbed in what they are doing. Returning to the concept of pilot hiring, the above attributes may be the requirements for future pilots to navigate current training methodologies. However, motivation, engagement, and many years of deliberate practice, identified as deliberate engagement, are essential to improving performance.[68]

Despite the difference between harmonious passion and obsessive passion, positive performance in an aircraft could be realized with either type of passion due to the amount of dedication and engagement in the job, be it pure enjoyment or the need for identity. However, a culture that promotes both engagement and harmonious passion will require performance feedback necessary for increased permanent wellbeing, and improved performance.[221] What happens to performance when pilots are not being paid to industry standards, who may be disgruntled due to work rules or lack of industry standards? Would a pilot make an effort to do more, learn more, and go beyond company requirements for knowledge acquisition? Would it be safe for the pilot to assume that if the airline believes what they are providing is enough for safe flight, and the FAA approves that program, there is no need to do more? An interesting statement was also made by an Atlas pilot, and could explain much of what's happening within that culture:

> *"Our biggest issue is lack of pay and poor morale. Our last 747 class hired 28, and only 7 showed."*
>
> *(Anonymous pilot)*

———————

Engagement tied to the passion of an AvGeek, may result in workers immersing themselves in their jobs, and could be the answer to improved performance. On the other hand, the disengaged pilot is not motivated and will detach from the job and be less motivated to self-study and learn beyond what is being provided in training. Engagement also relates to safety culture in reporting, learning, and informed cultures. This is where a pilot feels engaged to assist in improvements to procedures and overall safety of the system, and is free to report concerns to improve learning.

"I fly the Bombardier CRJ700 (70 Seats) for a regional airline. The aircraft has a glass instrumented Flight Deck but no Auto-Thrust system. We hand-fly the aircraft as much as possible below 10,000 feet and normally engage the AP before FL180 but definitely before FL290 due to RVSM automation requirements. We do this primarily because it's FUN! We know that someday we'll move on to a "mainline" carrier and fly an aircraft that wasn't even designed to have the pilot fly it except for 5 minutes during the takeoff and landing."

(Anonymous Pilot)

19. Literature Gap Review

THE GAP IN the literature prior to my research consisted of unanswered questions as to why pilots were not manually flying their aircraft and what was causing a lack of understanding, confusion, and mode awareness issues. Furthermore, whether the lack of understanding, confusion and mode awareness was influencing pilots' unwillingness to manually fly.

In current generation glass aircraft, manual flight does not dismiss the requirement of understanding operational modes or avoid the need to understand the data on the moving maps and instrumentation. This information does not disappear with the autopilot and autothrust disconnected. The pilot must understand and manage copious amounts of information.

Depending upon the definition, manual flight means that the pilot must be able to manually control the aircraft at the same time understand pitch, path, and speed modes in relation to performance required for the flight regime, as well as associated guidance for navigation and approach modes of operation. In a fly-by-wire aircraft, computers are still controlling some aspect of the aircraft and providing computer driven information to flight control surfaces during manual flight. Therefore, learning which buttons to push by rote memorization takes far less cognitive effort than manual flight, and perhaps less training, too. However, if the pilot does not understand the functionality of the automation or the information presented, disengaging the automation will only add to cognitive overload as the pilot will have to manage the aircraft in an unfamiliar system, within a dynamic environment. This lack of understanding, however, has been identified to be causal of accidents, incidents and pilot safety reports.

While improved understanding would naturally increase confidence, whether or not lack of systems understanding is the attributing factor to lack of confidence associated with manual flight is open for question. Training practices such as lack of manual flight in a simulator, lack of repetition, or lack of demonstrating the ability of manual flight with a training professional in the aircraft could diminish confidence and create the reluctance to disengage the automation.

Ample research has identified multiple factors of automation dependency; however, automation does not control the pilot. Unless corporate policy, or FAA regulations, mandate automation usage, the pilot has a choice. Thus, a question existed as to why pilots were choosing to not disengage the automation, despite FAA recommendations. The current question is, "could regulatory and corporate policy be hindering crew performance?" I believe that answer is yes.

A great deal of literature identifies how people learn, yet these learning practices are in conflict with approved training methodologies to include flash drive, train-at-home, ground schools, and simulated events that may only be experienced once under the AQP program. Learning takes repetition.

Industry officials have identified the problem—pilots lack flight skills, lack monitoring ability, and exhibit confusion in the aircraft. These issues have been identified as attributing factors to accidents and incidents. However, prior to my research there were questions as to why pilots were unwilling to manually fly, how the pilots' level of understanding impacted operational performance, and in what capacity training practices could be leaving pilots unwilling to manually fly their aircraft. These questions have now been answered.

Safety culture and training are impacting the level of understanding, all of which are operational performance. The questions have been answered, but will regulators solve the problem? That answer is yet to be determined.

20. Summary of Results

THE RESULTS HAVE identified that pilot understanding had the greatest influence on a pilot's willingness to manually fly the aircraft. The greatest influence on pilot understanding was pilot training. Pilot training also influenced manual flight, and safety culture had the greatest influence, by far, over pilot training. But the surprise of this research was—due to a negative safety culture, pilot training had a *negative* impact on manual flight.

It would appear obvious that pilot training would impact operational performance. This is how the pilots are trained. Equally obvious is the fact that an airline's culture would impact pilot training. The organization makes the rules, designs training programs, and implements procedures. What is most disconcerting with these results, however, is the negative influence pilot training had on manual flight as a result of safety culture.

The FAA and industry leaders have identified problems to be manual flight and lack of understanding. The FAA went as far to make a corrective action regarding the results of manual flight through a safety alert requiring airlines to encourage pilots to manually fly. Three years later, the Office of the Inspector General (OIG) reported pilots continue to lack hand-flying skills and lack monitoring ability. The question should be asked why did this FAA directive fail to improve the operational performance? The results in this study answer that question.

Airline culture is impacting pilot training which is removing pilots' willingness to manually fly.

Not only is encouragement to manually fly not taking hold, but the airlines are actually creating the reverse effect. Furthermore, "understanding" has been an ongoing issue identified to be the cause of accidents, incidents, and daily pilot reports. Understanding is a result of pilot training—now statistically proven— and the FAA has yet to address improvements to pilot training, assessment methods, or instructor training.

A more detailed explanation of the results is found in Appendix 1, including hypotheses testing and responses to all questions. However, the following is a summation of what we learned from these results as to how organization pilot training contradicts best practices of learning:

→ Learning by rote memorization— Per the results, 43% of the pilots queried utilize rote memorization practices.

→ Inadequate brief times— Per the results, 62% of the pilots queried received a 30-minutes or less debrief.

→ Lack of video during debrief— Per the results, 85% of the pilots queried were not recorded on a video.

→ Inadequate training materials— Per the results, 80% of the pilots queried utilized supplemental material (not provide by the company) with 50% stating this self-gathered material was necessary.

Approved training programs that may be inadequate, non-compliant, or recommendations not followed by operators that could be influencing training and understanding include:

+ Inadequate assessment measures. Per the results, 39% of the pilots queried received only an electronic or written assessment.

+ Lack of crew complement. Per the results, 50% of the pilots queried did not have the correct crew complement during training.

+ Lack of a standard taxonomy for manual flight. Per the results, the pilots disagreed as to the meaning of manual flight with 15% of the pilots queried believing it was only the autopilot disconnected, 49% of the pilots queried believed both the autopilot and autothrust must be disengaged, and 36% of the pilots queried believed that in addition to autopilot and autothrust being disconnected, that the manual flight also meant no use of the fight director.

+ Lack of flight line teaching without both the autopilot and autothrust. Per the results in the non-SEM questions, 32% of the instructors did not request the pilot to disengage the automation during training, and the SEM results identified 45% of the instructors did not encourage the pilots to disengage the automation.

Safety culture is the essence of the corporation's culture in that behaviors, values, beliefs, and how the organization does business relative to safety and associated processes, to include communication, reporting, flexibility, information sharing, and improvement strategies. Safety culture has greatest influence over the ultimate impact on pilots' decision to manually fly. Results indicate that all areas of safety culture could be improved upon, to include:

- ✈ Reporting Culture: How likely are you to critique and report any aspect of your employer's training program if you perceive it as substandard? Per the results, 34% of the pilots queried were unsure or would not critique the training program.

- ✈ Informed Culture: How likely is it that your employer's leadership team in pilot training, involved in program development, has knowledge of how humans learn and is aware of technology to improve learning? Per the results, 41% of the pilots queried were unsure or believed that management involved in training did not have expertise.

- ✈ Learning Culture: How likely is it that employee suggestions are taken into consideration by your employer? Per the results, 54% of the pilots queried were unsure or believed they would not be taken into consideration.

- ✈ Just Culture: How likely are you to agree with the following statement—the best way to have a successful career as a pilot, is to keep quiet and not make waves? Per the results, 54% of the pilots queried were unsure or believed it was best to keep quiet.

- ✈ Flexible Culture: How likely is it that your employer will exceed minimum regulatory compliance? Per the results, 46% of the pilots queried were unsure or believed their employer would not exceed regulatory compliance.

The greatest issues with pilot training were the lack of repetition:

✈ 39% of the pilots queried did not repeat event sets in direct opposition to learning.

Rote memorization was another highlight issue, in direct opposition to understanding:

✈ 69% of the pilots utilized rote memorization in systems training.

✈ 57% of the pilots utilized rote memorization in simulator training.

Feedback was positive:

✈ 74% of the pilots assessed received feedback.

Aviation passion was assessed and while the results identified a group that was overall passionate, the results reported the dispassionate perspective:

✈ 38% do not socialize with other aviators.

✈ 28% do not read aviation books or other aviation reading material.

✈ 32% do not purchase aviation themed products.

✈ 65% did not attend aviation events.

✈ 37% of the pilots were flying over 700 hours annually.

✈ 19% do not feel proud to be a pilot.

The high flight hours could indicate a time issue to attend aviation events, as well as the expense. And a future question regarding pride could also be asked, "Did you ever feel proud?"

Aviation industry officials, regulatory and management alike, have known for years what has been contributing to accidents, incidents, and safety reports. This research provided the data identifying a negative safety culture and associated training methodologies as the core of our industry problems Statistically speaking, what do you think they will do?

21. RECOMMENDATIONS

RECOMMENDATIONS WAS A required section in the dissertation and fell within three areas: future research, operational practice, and regulatory reform. Operational suggestions were expanded into two categories—pilot training with resultant understanding, and safety culture—the most significant factors impacting how pilots operate their aircraft. The recommendations presented in this text will focus only on operational practice and regulatory reform. Anyone planning to conduct future research, should locate the dissertation.

Operational Practice

IMPROVEMENTS MUST INCLUDE addressing pilot training and safety culture, as both are directly impacting operational practices.

Recommendations to improve training. Pilot training could be improved by employing SMEs who understand how people learn to develop training programs and redesign the training process based upon learning principles. Results identified that 41% of the crews queried believed those designing programs did not have experience to do so. The results of this research have identified this to be a sound opinion. Therefore, applying safety management systems

(SMS) to the training programs to incorporate risk mitigation and proactive safety measures could ensure pilots are trained to the level of understanding to operate the aircraft in a safe and efficient manner.

The following improvements to training practices could be realized:

✈ Restructure current training practices to include principles as to how pilots learn through repetition, feedback, and understanding.

✈ While a traditional classroom is ideal, the next best option is a virtual classroom with subject matter experts available to ensure understanding versus rote memorization.

✈ Follow FAA and ICAO mandates to ensure crew complement for all AQP operators.

✈ Reduce the training scenarios to three consecutive hours, with more training scenarios.

✈ Ensure instructors are trained how to assess and evaluate to include the elements of how to provide feedback to improve understanding and associated learning.

Recommendations to improve safety culture. Organizations worldwide are participating in SMS and US airlines are mandated to have an SMS program. However, without a safety culture as the foundation, SMS will be ineffective. Safety culture has been identified to significantly influence training with resultant performance, and therefore has a direct relationship to the safe operation.

Recommendations to improve safety culture based, upon the results identified include:

→ Assess the culture of the organization and based upon results, consider employing an outside organization to assist in a cultural shift.

→ Remove management who oppose a safety culture. As Collins purports—*who first, then what.*[40] A shift in culture does not have to be a lengthy process if positive action prevails by removing the players that participate in a negative culture. Leaving such players in place, and attempting to change the culture, will fall flat as the employees will not believe in the change. If management, who knowingly violate a reporting culture, violated policy, or violate FAR's, etc., are allowed to retire and receive financial benefits in the process, culture will never change. The message to employees will be it's okay to climb the ladder by violating policy and impact safety, because the worst that will happen is you will retire with a windfall. CEO's must fire these types of employees, but also communicate to the entire organization as to why the management shift—It's not okay to violate safety culture.

Regulatory Compliance

RESULTS IDENTIFY THAT organizations do not have a safety culture to support an SMS. Therefore, SMS will not be effective and operational safety will be a continued concern. Results identified that safety culture impacts training, understanding, and how pilots manually fly, and airlines' worldwide lack of a positive safety culture worldwide. Safety culture issues that should be addressed include:

→ An informed culture should dictate a worldwide taxonomy for manual flight. Operators should inform and educate employees as to the type of required training (AQP or not) and required operating practices. The only way employees can accurately assess and critique their training programs is by having knowledge of what is required, and 36% have no knowledge of training requirements.

✈ Modifications to the Wendell H. Ford Aviation Investment and Reform Act for the 21st Century (AIR21) should be considered due to lack of a reporting culture. An Air 21 is the whistleblower act that is supposed to protect employees from retaliation when they bring safety related concerns forward. Currently this process, perhaps not intentional, makes it extremely difficult for an employee to persevere under the current design. Therefore protection is in question. Not only a restructuring of the process is necessary, but a punitive approach toward offenders who violate a just and reporting culture would send the message to operators worldwide that retaliation is not accepted when an employee reports an unsafe act.

Until organizations feel a financial impact and the negative publicity of their actions, counterproductive to safety, safety culture will continue to be a problem, SMS will fail, and the negative influence on pilot training and operational practices will continue.

22. Conclusion

THE FAA, INDUSTRY reports, and literature review identified the problem that assisted in developing this study. However, during the preliminary stage of this research, SMEs were queried to help ascertain what was occurring on the flight line in regard to manual flight. I wanted to know what the line check airman thought. These are the pilots designated by the FAA to conduct training and checking events. An FAA designee on the Airbus A330, at an international airline, supported industry concerns when he stated that pilots were not manually flying because of, "Lack of confidence" "Lack of proficiency" and "Fear."

An example of manual flight performance is further represented by the action of a U.S. international airline captain after he experienced a systems failure during departure which prevented the engagement of the autopilot and autothrust. He flew into RVSM airspace, where reduced vertical separation mandates an operational autopilot, continued to destination, and then declared an emergency in VFR (visual) conditions when ATC would not provide a block altitude for arrival, simply because he did not have an autopilot. He said, "To have my skills degrade to a point where a level 0 VMC landing in [Airport] required declaring an emergency is a personal wake-up call. I hate to think that someday manual flight operations will be an assumed emergency, but that day may be approaching."

When the initial cadre of experienced instructors at a U.S. airline (many had Airbus experience) were learning the Airbus A350 systems (a highly automated aircraft) via a computer-based training program, and 100% failed one or more system modules, the efficacy of a CBT training program that required pilots to listen to audio online, support the results of current training programs that may be deficit and are influencing pilots' level of understanding. Furthermore, the captain who declared the emergency, due to the loss of the auto flight system, lacked knowledge that he was prohibited from operating in RVSM airspace. He was also not provided that information from ground operations, indicative of either a lack of understanding by all, or lack of information sharing, both of which are required with an informed culture. Safety culture is the foundation of an SMS, and this research has identified that safety culture worldwide is impacting how pilots operate their aircraft.

Safety culture has the greatest impact on pilot training, therefore, is the underlying factor with the greatest influence as to how pilots learn and operate their aircraft. The captain who declared the emergency in the above example, is also the head of human factors and analyzes ASAP reports and further stated, "We as a group are presently not prepared to fly in complex airspace with Level 0 automation. Nor, might I add, are we suitably prepared to fly in complex airspace with Level 4 automation (so says ASAP)." Furthermore, this airline's internal response to the identification of this global flight performance issue was not to improve training, but to encourage pilots to declare an emergency if they lost their automation under the construct of workload management.

The Office of the Inspector General identified that pilots' lacked flight skills and exhibited problems monitoring their instruments, and incidents and safety reports have further identified confusion, lack of understanding, and mode awareness issues contributing to accidents and incidents worldwide. I hypothesized that pilots were not to blame, but a larger system with underlying variables could be attributing factors. The questions have been answered by statistical analysis, now it is up to the operators and regulators to utilize this information to improve safety.

> *"The world is a dangerous place, not because*
> *of those who do evil, but those who sit back*
> *and do nothing."*
>
> Albert Einstein

Despite training practices, culture, or events beyond the pilot's control, at the end of the day pilots hold the responsibility of professionalism. While this research identified areas of concern at the hand of management that are ultimately influencing aviation safety, a comment I received sums up the pilot's responsibility:

"A message I received from listening to Dr. Tony Kern speak, and is emphasized in his books, is one that I live by—Don't worry about what your company might be pushing or the fact that you can get away with less than 100% effort much of the time. You owe it to yourself to always do your best, because today could be the day that you need to fly to the limit of your ability."

(Anonymous Pilot)

Appendix 1 Results

THE PURPOSE OF this research was necessary to gather the data to narrow the gap between operational practice and current research dealing with aviator performance related to automation usage. Whereas current literature addresses pilot fatigue, automation challenges, situation awareness, safety culture, confidence, and learning methodologies, there continues to be a gap between real world operational problems and current research. My contention is, if you want to know the answer to the problem, you must first ask the question. The following results identify how 7491 pilots responded.

Demographics

Seat Position:

Captain: 52%
First Officer: 42%
Cruise Pilot: 1%
Between job: 2%
Retired: 3%

Age:

21-35 years old: 9%
36-40 years old: 14%
41-45 years old: 13%
46-50 years old: 13%
51-55 years old: 12%
56-60 years old: 9%
61-65 years old: 5%

Gender:

> Male: 91%
> Female: 9%

Current employer:

> Major Airline: 70%
> Regional Airline: 16%
> Fractional/corporate: 10%
> Charter: 7%

Corporate headquarters:

United States: 44%

Europe: 24.5%

Asia, Australia/Oceanic:17.5%

Operating Experience

Instructor/check airman experience:

62% Yes.

Total flight time:

> 5000-1000 hours: 26%
> > 10,000 hours: 45%

Recreational flight hours:

100-400 and 2% 400-700

Primary job flight hours the previous 12 months:

> 40% 401-700
> 35% 701-1000

Aircraft Type:

> 42% Boeing
> 28% Airbus

Glass Cockpit:

92%

Type of Flying:

> 73% short-haul
> 27% long-haul

Initial Training:

> 11% Air force
> 4% Navy/Marine/Coast Guard
> 44% General Aviation
> 1% Army
> 37% Flight College

Time since initial training:

> < 1 year 22%;
> 1-3 years 29%;
> 3-5 years: 17%;
> 5-10 years 16%;
> >10 years 16%

Hypothesis Testing Manual Flight

STRUCTURAL EQUATION MODELS were built for each of the factors—and AMOS, a statistical analysis program, was utilized to assess the relationships. The relationships were identified by regression weights. The larger the number (regression weight) the greater the influence as compared to the other factors. A negative number identifies a negative influence.

Each of these assessments were a multivariate analysis versus a univariate analysis, meaning that all factors were included when assessing a relationship. A univariate analysis would not include the other factors. In that nothing happens in isolation the models controlled for all factors, and the reason all hypotheses state "controlling for" the other factors. When dependent variable is addressed, this is the variable that is being impacted by the other factors.

Manual Flight Assessment

MULTIVARIATE ANALYSIS WITH manual flight as the dependent variable identified the most influential factor was Pilot Understanding (PU) with a pilot's willingness to manually fly the aircraft. Aviation Passion (AP) was the second most influential. Pilot Training (PT) had a negative influence. Safety Culture (SC) presented a small effect. All results indicated an influence.

Standardized regression weights:

> PU= .28
> PT = -.10
> AP = .15
> SC =.06.

WITH MANUAL FLIGHT as the dependent variable the results confirmed that all relationships with Pilot Understanding, Pilot Training, Aviation Passion, and Safety Culture, were significant. The following hypotheses, $H_{1A,}$ $H_{3A,}$ and $H_{4A,}$ are supported because they were positive. While H_{2A} indicated an influence, this influence identified a negative relationship between training and a pilot's willingness to manually fly, therefore was not supported. To clarify the results for the non-statisticians, I will add a statement after each hypothesis to articulator if the hypothesis was supported. What this means is, did the results identify the statement to be true or not.

Hypotheses 1-4

$H_{1A:}$ Pilots' aircraft understanding positively influences willingness to manually fly, controlling for pilot training, aviation passion and safety culture. This was a proven to be a true statement.

$H_{2A:}$ Training positively influences willingness to manually fly, controlling for pilot understanding, aviation passion and safety culture. This was proven *not* to be a true statement because of the negative results. This was significant, but negative, meaning, training negatively influences a pilot's willingness to manually fly.

$H_{3A:}$ Aviation passion positively influences pilots' willingness to manually fly, controlling for pilot training, safety culture and understanding. This was proven to be a true statement.

$H_{4A:}$ Safety culture positively influences pilots' willingness to manually fly, controlling for pilot training, aviation passion and understanding. This was proven to be a true statement.

Pilot Training Assessment

MULTIVARIATE ANALYSIS WITH Pilot Training as the dependent variable identified all results were significant. The most influential factor impacting pilot training was Safety Culture (SC). Pilot Understanding (PU) was second. However, Aviation Passion (AP) and Manual Flight (MF) both presented a negative relationship.

Standardized regression weights:

SC= .54
PU=.25
AP= -.122
MF= -067

With pilot training as the dependent variable, safety culture and pilot understanding were both identified to influence pilot training. However, aviation passion and manual flight while significant both negatively influenced pilot training.

Hypotheses 5-8

$H_{5A:}$ Safety culture positively influences pilot training, controlling for manual flight, aviation passion and understanding. This was proven to be a true statement.

$H_{6A:}$ Aviation passion positively influences pilot training, controlling for manual flight, safety culture and pilot understanding. This was proven *not* to be a true statement because of the negative results. This was significant, but negative, meaning if a pilot has aviation passion this passion negatively influences the pilot training process. If the training processes deny manual flight, this could explain this negative impact.

$H_{7A:}$ Pilot understanding positively influences pilot training, controlling for aviation passion, manual flight, and safety culture. This was proven to be a true statement.

H_{8A} : Manual flight positively influences pilot training, controlling for aviation passion, understanding, and safety culture. This was proven *not* to be a true statement because of the negative results. This was significant, but negative, meaning if a pilot prefers to manually fly, this behavior negatively influences the pilot training process. A training program that denies the ability to manual fly would present an opposing effect with manual flight upon training.

Pilot Understanding Assessment

WITH PILOT UNDERSTANDING as the dependent all results were significant, and all positive. The most influential factor over Pilot Understanding was Pilot Training. Manual Flight and Safety Culture presented the next greatest influence and were the same number, and Aviation Passion slightly less.

Standardized regression weights:
    PT = .27
    MF = .21
    SC = .21
    AP = .20

Pilot Understanding confirmed that all relationships were significant and all supported. All factors were similar as to the influence on Pilot Understanding, with Pilot Training showing the greatest influence.

Hypotheses 9-12

$H_{9A:}$ Safety culture positively influences pilot understanding, controlling for manual flight, aviation passion and pilot training. This was proven to be a true statement.

$H_{10A:}$ Aviation passion positively influences pilot understanding, controlling for manual flight, safety culture and pilot training. This was proven to be a true statement.

$H_{11A:}$ Pilot training positively influences pilot understanding, controlling for aviation passion, manual flight, and safety culture. This was proven to be a true statement.

$H_{12A:}$ Manual flight positively influences understanding, controlling for aviation passion, pilot training, and safety culture. This was proven to be a true statement.

Mediation hypothesis.

A MEDIATION PATH model was built to determine the total effect of Pilot Training would have on Manual Flight as impacted by Safety Culture. I was curious if the negative effect of pilot training on manual flight was a result of safety culture. Testing for a mediation hypothesis was a four-step process, that can be viewed in the dissertation. However, results identified that Safety Culture was negatively impacting the positive effect that Pilot Training had on Manual Flight.

Analysis of the mediating model identified there was a mediating effect, but this was a negative effect. What this indicates is that Safety Culture is removing a positive relationship that Pilot Training directly had on Manual Flight. This process identified that in isolation, pilot training did have a small but positive influence on manual flight decisions; whereas in the multivariate analysis pilot training had a negative effect on manual flight. These results identify that safety culture is removing the positive influence pilot training could have on a pilot's decision to manually fly.

Hypothesis 13

$H_{13A:}$ Safety culture positively influences pilot training, which influences a pilot's willingness to manually fly. This was proven *not* to be a true statement because of the negative results. This means that safety culture is removing any positive influence that pilot training could have on a pilot's willingness to manually fly,

SEM questions

THE FOLLOWING SECTION, identified by the factors, is a summation of the results from the questions that were utilized with the structural equation model (SEM), to support or not-support the hypotheses. Despite the results presented above with the standardized regression weights, the following information will provide a clear picture with the percentages of how 5661 pilots responded.

Manual flight questions. The manual flight SEM questions identified the likelihood of automation usage in different phases of flight. Overall, 27-30% of the population are not likely to disengage the autopilot and autothrust at any given time, and more than 50% will not disengage prior to the final approach phase and more than half would not disengage the flight director. These results identify that pilots are utilizing automation more than they are manual flying, and pilot comments reflect that this decision could be primarily due to company policy, written and unwritten, versus personal choice.

Pilot understanding questions. A seven-point Likert scale was utilized for the SEM opinion and operational based questions, which enabled pilots to answer knowledge-based questions on a level from extremely unlikely to extremely likely versus an absolute. The assumption was, if the pilot absolutely knew the systems question, they would select extremely likely (7). However, anything below extremely likely would indicate doubt of absolute knowledge, indicating they might not have the necessary level of understanding. Predicated on the assumption that extremely likely identified knowledge, the participants responses identified that 21% were certain they understood the flight management system, 36% understood the flight mode annunciator, but only 7% were sure they could pass an oral without studying, only 9% could handle an emergency without direction, and 12% understood why the procedure was written. These results indicate that pilots may lack understanding of the equipment they fly and operational practices.

Pilot training questions. A key factor that could be influencing learning is the high percentage of pilots utilizing rote memorization versus understanding, in that 61% utilized rote memorization in ground school and 57% in simulator training. In this series of questions, of the pilots surveyed 73% reported they received feedback and 79% were allowed self-assessment. Only 55% of pilots queried were encouraged by a check airmen to manually fly during OE. Lack of repetition identified that 39% of the pilots questioned did not repeat event sets.

Safety culture questions. The FAA defines safety culture as, "the shared values, actions, and behaviors that demonstrate a commitment to safety over competing goals and demands," and comprises five sub cultures—reporting, just, flexible, informed, and learning (FAA, 2013b, p. 9). Safety culture is the essence of an organizations culture, and identified by behavior that stems, in part, from beliefs and underlying assumptions, and is an influential factor in manual flight and pilot training.

Overall 54% of the population was unsure or did not believe their suggestions would be taken into consideration, 34% were unsure or unlikely to critique their training program, 41% lacked a belief or were unsure if the leadership in charge of developing training programs had the expertise of learning, 54% were unsure or believed it was best to keep quiet, and 46% were unsure or did not believe their company would exceed regulatory compliance. These results identify that organizations worldwide may lack a positive safety culture.

Aviation passion questions. Aviation passion in this study refers to an individual's involvement in aviation activity beyond work experience, such as recreational flight, aviation club participation, reading aviation magazines and books, flying home simulators, or purchasing aviation themed products. Overall the population appeared to have a strong level of passion, in that 35% were likely to attend an aviation event, 68% were likely to purchase an aviation themed product, 72% were likely to read aviation themed books, 62% were likely to socialize with other aviators outside work, and 81% of them were proud to be pilots.

Pilot Opinion Questions

PERFORMANCE IDENTIFIED IN this research is the level of automation utilized during flight. The FAA and worldwide civil aviation authorities operate under approved training programs and assessment methods. However, results indicate that these programs may not be effective for learning and assessing performance. While policy dictates standard operating procedures; the results identified that 69% of the participants reported their organization had unwritten policies regarding automation usage. The entire survey and results can be located in the dissertation but what follows is a discussion of the opinion-based questions.

Manual flight. The results identified there was confusion as to what constitutes manual flight, whereas 15% of the participants believe that manual flight is when only the autopilot is disconnected, 49% believe both the autopilot and autothrust must be disconnect, and 36% believe that manual flight means that the autopilot, autothrust, and the flight director must be disengaged. This confusion is not unfounded, as there is a taxonomy difference between the OIG and the FAA.

Automation preference. Pilots reported their preference was to fly with the autopilot and autothrust connected by 74% and 78% respectively. The presentation of the ensuing responses to the opinion-based questions assist in understanding this preference.

Automation opinion. This series of questions were written as dichotomous questions despite each answer being contingent upon other variables—mental fatigue, physical fatigue, overall flying experience, experience of fellow crewmembers, experience of the active arrival or location, cognitive ability, inter crewmember tension or conflict, life stress, pilot age, weather, location of flight, time of flight, time of crewmember's break, quality of crew rest, passenger issues, recency of training, length of flight, circadian rhythm, or any combination of these variables, or others. Adding the option, "it depends" would have resulted with all participants selecting the option it depends, because it does.

Safety, overload, confusion, risk, complexity, and situation awareness are not absolutes, and all move along a spectrum of "more" or "less" dependent upon other factors. With this in mind, the following responses provide an overall perception of what pilots think about automation without any conditional factors included.

These experiential responses are reflective of the individual's type of flying, and therefore will portray an authentic belief based upon that experience. A domestic short-haul pilot that flies into the same airport multiple times daily, will not have the experience to make an accurate response to a more detailed question, such as to the necessity of automation after a long-haul flight, with an augmented crew, flying into a foreign country, after being on duty for 15 hours, but could only answer based upon an assumption. Allowing pilots to answer with the mindset of their daily experience was assumed to provide the most authentic responses.

Automation is safer than manual flight. Results identified that 75% of the population believe that automated flight is safer than manual flight. Automation is safer when the automation works, the pilot understands how to use it, and there are no extenuating circumstances. However, participant's comments indicated automation may be safer due to the lack of manual flight ability, and they do not necessarily agree that fully automated flight is in the best interest of overall safety, despite being safer.

Manual flight overloads the pilot flying. Results identified that 49% of the participants believe that manual flight overloads the pilot monitoring, where 51% believe it does not. The differences in these responses would be contingent upon a number of variables such as operations in a foreign country or airport, complexity of the arrival, ATC involvement, and airport conditions. Therefore, the split difference was varied per the pilot's operating environment. Pilot comments further identified the complexity of manual flight and the decision to manually fly could be based upon overload and complexity of the air traffic system more so than the aircraft.

Manual flight reduces situation awareness. Results identified that 51% of the participants believe that manual flight reduces situation awareness, meaning that 49% believe they can remain situationally aware while manually flying the aircraft. The response to this question is one that is also situational. During high workload, higher levels of automation usage has been identified to improve situation awareness, yet when mental workload is increased due to lack of understanding of complex aircraft systems, operations, or interpreting the automation, higher levels of automation will reduce situation awareness. In addition, the fact that pilots have a different perception of what manual flight means, would impact the response to this question. A pilot who believes that manual flight is all automation disengaged (autopilot, autothrust and flight director) would believe this to reduce situation awareness more so than simply the autopilot. Concern for situation awareness when something fails on the aircraft was identified in the pilot comments.

Manual flight and the risk of violations. Research has identified that flight skill retention in automated aircraft was determined to remain relatively intact without consistent performance, yet degradation of cognitive ability necessary for manual flight was apparent. Results indicated that 61% of participants believe that manual flight exposes the pilot to more risk, could be explained by these results. Without manual flight skill retention, due to lack of practice, there will be an increased potential for error with an ensuing violation.

Fly by wire and automation complexity. The focus of automation research has revolved around flight deck displays of a glass cockpit and integrated system designs with limited discussion on flight control operations and understanding the complexity of the fly-by-wire system. Pilots' lack of understanding, poor attention, limited knowledge, mode awareness issues, and problems managing an automation surprise have been identified to be resultant from automation complexity. It is also believed that automation creates more confusion for the pilot due to complexity. However, of the pilots queried, most of which are operating these complex, highly automated fly-by-wire aircraft, state a different opinion than the aircraft complexity theory.

Results identified that participants believe that the fly-by-wire aircraft were meant to be manually flown and were not too complex for manual flight by 71% and 95% respectively, and 91% did not believe fly by wire aircraft were confusing.

Company policy. Corporate culture plays a key role in pilots' performance beyond espoused values, corporate rules, and written procedures, in that the unwritten rules are what often guide behavior and influence performance. Corporate culture therefore extends to performance in how the airline culture behaves and transcends to employee performance standards. As reported through pilot comments worldwide, there are a variety of policies regarding automation usage, both written and unwritten. Results identified that unwritten policies are more prevalent than the written policy regarding mandates to utilize automation.

Written policies. Unless corporate policy or civil aviation authority regulations mandate automation usage, the pilot has a choice. Thus, a question as to why pilots are choosing not to disengage the automation, despite FAA recommendations are answered with these results. Results identified that 56% of the participants state that the company has written policies mandating automation usage. However, all carriers operating automated aircraft for hire have policies regarding automation. In that only 7% of the population did not fly an automated aircraft, this response rate could be due to confusion as to the term *automation policies*, similar to the confusion of the term manual flight, and contingent upon understanding the question. English as a second language was identified as a limitation in this research and could be attributed with this response. Comments on automation usage appear to be varied indicating autopilot, autothrust and flight director policies are company specific as identified by pilot comments.

Unwritten policies. Whereas 56% of the participants stated their company had written policies mandating automation usage, 69% stated their company has unwritten policies mandating automation usage. The FAA's recommendation for manual flight, disconnecting both autopilot and autothrust, and the companies' perceived compliance via written policy versus how they actually advise the pilots to operate through unwritten policies are identified in the various pilot comments. The company states one thing in writing, but unwritten policies dictate an operational reality.

The response to the discernment between unwritten policies and practice could be found in the definition of corporate culture being a pattern of behavior stemming from, in part, espoused values, beliefs, and underlying assumptions, in addition to policies and procedures, which all include elements of a safety culture.[222]

Performance. Performance in this research is referenced as to the level of automation the pilot chooses to utilize. In response to how pilots operate related to automation usage and their preference for the other pilot, 71% of the pilots monitoring prefer the pilot flying utilize automation, and 58% state that the pilots they fly with rarely, if ever, fly without the autopilot or autothrust engaged.

Training. A preponderance of research and accident investigations attributed automation-related pilot errors, in part, to inadequate training, with sub-optimal training as one of the two most significant flight hazards. Training questions encompassed necessity for supplemental training aids, type of ground school and assessment measures, participant's recency, companies training cycle, debriefing time, self-assessment during the brief and the use of a video, AQP certification, how the pilot studied to pass the oral examination, manual flight during operating experience (OE) and crew complement during training.

Supplemental training. The question as to whether pilots are being provided the tools in their respective companies regarding training was identified as 80% of the pilots queried utilized additional information to learn the aircraft and 50% of those pilots stated that additional information was necessary in order to pass training, These results indicate that operators are not providing adequate resources to navigate their training program, and better yet to learn their aircraft.

Type of ground school. Regulatory agencies have enabled airlines to cancel traditional ground-schools, where pilots are no longer mandated to come together in a classroom environment with an instructor and fellow classmates to learn aircraft operating systems. Under AQP, airline flight operations management have been authorized to allow pilots to teach themselves aircraft systems and computer operations via at-home training programs. This training process relies upon an assumption that pilots will acquire correct systems understanding, and when an inflight emergency arises the pilot will have accurate knowledge to deal with it. Responses identified those with a classroom and instructor represented 24%, whereas completely self-taught were 13%, and a combination of self-taught and classroom represented 63%. However, comments identified that the combination of both could be reflective of self-taught followed by a review.

Type of systems evaluation. Training assessment has been an ongoing challenge, yet, until recently, little research existed on effective simulator training evaluation measures. However, effective evaluation is the only way to determine training program effectiveness. Pilot performance, as identified by accidents, incidents, and ASRS may be better indicators of training effectiveness than current AQP data collection processes during simulator training events, and electronic reviews.

Furthermore, accepted training assessment processes do not necessarily substantiate that learning has taken place in the form of understanding and retention, with the capability to transfer that knowledge to the aircraft. Results depicts that 39% of participants took a written or electronic systems test, 8% took a systems oral, and 53% stated they took a combination of both. It was identified that the potential of "both" was due to a self-study program followed by a review of the systems test.

Recency and recurrent training cycle. A recency event is a simulator training event where a pilot performs three takeoffs and landings, within 90-days, to maintain currency per Federal Aviation Regulation (FAR) 121.439. Recurrent simulator training is a regulated event where pilots will receive an approved number of simulator days for training and evaluation, conducted on either a sixth month, nine month, or annual cycle. There is no requirement for knowledge assessment during pilot recency or recurrent training events beyond rote memorization of limitations or memory items, and no requirements for repetition or practice of manual flight skills. Results identified that the majority of participants were actively flying and 65% rarely or ever required a recency, 20% needed a recency twice per year, 10% once a year and 5% visited the simulator three times per year to maintain proficiency. In addition, 57% of the pilots attended a 6-month cycle, 17% every 9 months, and 23% annually. This indicated that the majority of the pilots were able to maintain currency on the flight line.

Average debriefing time. The power of the flight crew debrief has been the focus of much research and is instrumental in how pilots learn from human error. Results identified that 13% of the pilots spent less than 15 minutes in a debrief, 49% spent 15 to 30 minutes, and 33 % spent 31 to 60 minutes, whereas 4% spent over 60 minutes. As identified in comments, one participant reported they were forced to select less than 15 minutes but never received any debrief.

Debrief self-assessment. Automated aircraft provide extensive latitude for safety, meaning there is a great deal of room for error as automation is a safety net that minimizes consequences of pilot performance. Thus, pilots have the opportunity to perform and respond to mismanaged arrivals, poor decision-making, and lack of SA without resulting in a consequential event. This self-assessment includes both on the flight line and in the simulator. Results identified that 87% of the pilots were able to self-assess and reflect upon their training experience during their debriefing session.

Oral preparation. How a pilot learns the aircraft between understanding versus memorizing facts will be reflective of operational performance. Rote memorization does not guarantee the pilot understands the system. When asked how the pilots prepare to pass a systems validation, 43% stated they learned by memorizing facts, where 57% learned the aircraft to understand systems and processes. These results identify that close to half the pilot population may have limited understanding due to memorized procedures that may not transfer to the aircraft beyond events practiced and anticipated in the simulator.

Manual flight operating experience. Results identified that 68% of the pilots were allowed to disengage the autopilot and autothrottle during operating experience (OE). Therefore 32% were not allowed to disengage the automation, despite a checkairman on the aircraft. Without the ability to disengage the automation with an instructor onboard, the chance the pilots will have confidence to do this on their own is unlikely.

AQP certification. AQP is a train to proficiency program that mandates inclusion of CRM, LOFT, and line operational evaluation (LOE) scenarios. AQP simulator training requires a myriad of mandates. If the pilots do not know if they are training under an AQP program, they will have no knowledge if the airline is following required protocol. Results identified that 48% of the participants reported their company was AQP certified, 16% were not, and 36% were unsure. The high response of those who are unsure identifies a culture issue relating to the lack of an informed culture, and an associated limited knowledge of training requirements. Unfortunately, FAA regulators overseeing airline's training programs may lack knowledge as well. During my research I spoke to an FAA inspector who had been with the FAA since his retirement at sixty years of age. We had worked with at a previous airline in the training department. I spoke of AQP and he stated, "I don't know anything about AQP because AQP didn't arrive until I retired." The irony of this statement was—he is responsible for overseeing an airline that has an AQP program.

Video. When students observe their performance utilizing a video, and self-assessment and reflection are done with an instructor and peers, maximum performance gains can be realized (170). The utilization of a video is not a requirement for AQP, but could be effective tool for collecting proficiency data, and assisting with the debrief as this process is a highly efficient and cost-effective tool that could improve training effectiveness. When queried as to the use of this tool, 85% of the population stated they were not videotaped during training.

Crew complement. A crew complement is required under AQP. In part, justification to reduce the number of required simulator sessions was due to pilots being trained and assessed as a crew, where half the training and assessment was being conducted as the pilot monitoring and the other half as the pilot flying. Therefore, training must occur in the pilot's respective seat. A first officer's pilot monitoring training must be conducted in the first officer seat, as there are additional responsibilities that must be learned and practiced. Results identified that 50% of the training is not being conducted as a crew, whereas only 15% of the pilots reported their training was not AQP certified. Once again, if the FAA doesn't know the mandate, who will ensure the compliance?

DEFINITIONS

Adaptive expertise. Adaptive expertise is where understanding and contextual-based knowledge, combined with motivation for problem solving, creates adaptive and flexible strategies for unexpected events (Bohle, Stalmeijer, Konings, Segers & Van Merrienboer, 2014).

Aeronautical Decision Making (ADM). ADM is "a systematic approach to the mental process used by pilots to consistently determine the best course of action in response to a given set of circumstances" (Federal Aviation Administration, 1991, p. 4).

AvGeek. "An AvGeek is someone who is passionate about aviation and that passion can be shown in countless ways" to include photography, aviation club participation, reading aviation magazines and books, flying home simulators, and/or owning aircraft models (Brown, 2013, par. 4).

Aviation passion. Passion is defined as "a strong inclination toward an activity that people like, find important and which they invest their time and energy" (Vallerand et.al., 2008 p. 1), whereas aviation passion is a passionate connection to aviation.

Aviation Safety Action Program (ASAP). *ASAP* is a pilot self-reporting program to encourage pilots to report information for system improvement without fear of disciplinary action (FAA, 2004b). The ASAP reports are directed to the pilots' airline.

Aviation Safety Reporting System (ASRS). The ASRS is a voluntary program that receives and analyzes incident reports that describe unsafe events and potential hazards, from "pilots, air traffic controllers, dispatchers, cabin crew, maintenance technicians, and others" to improve safety (NASA, 2015, p. 4). This report is submitted to NASA.

Automaticity. When a pilot's knowledge is at the level where he or she does not have to think about what to do, the response is automatic (Casner, Geven, & Williams, 2013).

Automation. For the purpose of this study, automation refers to a fully engaged auto-flight system, where the autopilot and authothrust are both engaged, and aircraft control is determined by parameters programed into the computer by the pilots, or with pilot mode control panel intervention as required per ATC commands (OIG, 2016).

Automation dependence. For the purpose of this study automation dependence is a pilot's reliance on both the autopilot and autothrust (Parasuraman & Wickens, 2008).

Cognitive architecture. Cognitive architecture is the framework representing the mind's structures and processes, related to working memory, information processing, and long-term memory storage (Sweller, van Merrienboer, & Paas, 1998).

Competency. For the purpose of this study, competency is "the consistent application of knowledge and skill to the standard of performance required in the workplace. It embodies the ability to transfer and apply skills and knowledge to new situations and environments" (Franks et al., 2014, p. 132).

Corporate culture. Corporate culture is a pattern of behavior stemming from artifacts, espoused values and beliefs, underlying assumptions, policies and procedures, to include elements of a safety culture, identifying organizational processes (Schein, 2010; Stolzer & Goglia, 2015).

Confidence. The pilot's belief that he or she will perform well, know what they are doing, and will succeed at a given action (Johnson, & Fowler, 2011).

Confusion. "A situation in which people are uncertain about what to do or are unable to understand something clearly; the feeling that you have when you do not understand what is happening, what is expected, etc.; a state or situation in which many things are happening in a way that is not controlled or orderly" (Confusion, n.d., para. 11).

Consciously competent. "The crew has the knowledge and skill to cope with the situation but must apply much effort to deal with it" (Besco, 1997, p. 60).

Consciously incompetent. "The crew knows what they don't know. This can occur when the crew is aware of the gravity of the problem but is unable to select suitable responses to the perceived situation" (Besco, 1997, p. 59).

Flexible culture. "People can adapt organizational processes when facing high temporary operations or certain kinds of danger, shifting from the conventional hierarchical mode to a flatter mode" (Stolzer & Goglia, 2015, p. 28).

Flight skill loss. For the purpose of this paper, flight skill loss refers to the reduction in manual flying skills.

Flight training. Training in a simulator or aircraft, other than ground training.

Fly-by-wire. The term used for an aircraft where electronic signals provide input to flight control surfaces versus cable driven control (Airbus, 2003).

Flight Operational Quality Assurance (FOQA). FOQA is a voluntary safety program that collects digital performance data during flight operations, enabling participating airlines to share de-identified data to identify operating trends in order to improve performance (FAA, 2004a).

Fractional Airline. An airline, such as NetJets, where the customers share ownership in the aircraft.

Full autoflight. Full autoflight indicates that both the autopilot and autothrust are engaged, and the aircraft is being flown per pilot programmed commands without mode control panel interventions (FAA, 2016; OIG, 2016).

Full manual flight. For the purpose of this research, full manual flight is where the pilot manually flies the aircraft without the authothrust, autopilot, and flight director engaged (OIG, 2016).

Glass cockpit. A flight deck with integrated electronic instrument displays versus analog digital flight instruments termed round-dial.

Harmonious passion. Harmonious passion is passion internalized into the individual's identity, where they are highly motivated and dedicated, and this passion is in harmony with their life (Kocjan, 2015).

Informed culture. "Those who manage and operate the system have current knowledge about human, technical, organizational and environmental factors that determine the safety of the system as a whole" (Gain, 2004, p. 4).

Initial flight training. Initial flight training is defined as qualification, and is the training program administered to pilots new to an aircraft, under the airline's approved program (FAA, 2017a).

Just culture. "A just culture refers to a way of safety thinking that promotes a questioning attitude, is resistant to complacency, is committed to excellence, and fosters both personal accountability and corporate self-regulation in safety matters" (Gain, 2004, p. 4).

Knowledge. For the purpose of this study, knowledge includes both declarative knowledge (factual knowledge the pilot has about the aircraft operating, annunciation, and navigation systems) and procedural knowledge (pilots know how to perform the company's standard operating procedures), pertaining to the aircraft and flight operations.

Learning culture. "Continuous improvement is a characteristic of a learning culture that enables proactive risk management through process improvement" (Yantiss, 2011, p. 169).

Legacy carrier. A legacy carrier is an airline that had an established route structure prior to the Deregulation Act of 1978 (Wensveen, 2011).

Level 0 automation. For the purposes of this paper, level 0 automation is manual flight, without any automation engaged (Aldana, 2013).

Level 1 automation. For the purposes of this paper, level 1 automation indicates that only the flight director is engaged, and the flight is being flown without autothrust or the autopilot and is considered manual flight for LOSA observations (FAA, 2013d).

Level 2 automation. For the purposes of this paper, level 2 automation indicates that the flight director and the autothrust are both engaged, yet the autopilot is disengaged, which is also considered manual flight per the OIG (OIG, 2016).

Level 3 automation. For the purpose of this paper, level 3 automation indicates that the flight director, autothrust, and autopilot are all engaged—termed full autoflight—yet performance parameter interventions are available to the pilot, also termed tactical autoflight (OIG, 2016).

Level 4 automation. Level 4 automations is a fully automated aircraft, with the flight director, autothrust, and autopilot engaged, and the aircraft is being flown per programmed commands without mode control panel interventions—the concept of NextGen operations (Aldana, 2013; FAA, 2016; OIG, 2016).

Line Check Safety Audit (LCSA). "LCSA is an event in which a check airman occupying the jump seat observes a flight crew in the operation of an aircraft" (Esser, 2005, p. 8).

Line Operational Evaluation (LOE). "LOE is an evaluation of individual and crew performance in a flight simulation device conducted during real-time. LOE is primarily designed in accordance with an approved design methodology for crewmember evaluation under an AQP" (FAA, 2004b, p.iii).

Line Oriented Flight Training (LOFT). "LOFT is conducted as a line operation and allows for no interruption by the instructor during the session except for a non-disruptive acceleration of uneventful enroute segments" (FAA, 2004b, pii). A LOFT can either be an initial qualification LOFT, or a recurrent LOFT.

Line Operations Safety Audit (LOSA). "LOSA is an event in which a trained individual occupying the jump seat observes a flight crew in the operation of an aircraft" (Esser, 2005. p. 8).

Manual flight. For the purpose of this research manual flight is where the pilot manually flies the aircraft without the authothrust and autopilot engaged (OIG, 2016).

Mode Awareness. "Awareness of aircraft configuration and auto flight system modes. The latter includes such aspects as current and target speed, altitude, heading, AP/FD armed/engaged modes and the state of flight management system (FMS) data entries" (Airbus, 2007, p. 1).

Network driven sampling. A term utilized in this research to identify a non-random sampling method that is a hybrid of purposive sampling, snowball sampling and respondent driven sampling, where I am a member of population that does not have a sampling frame, and relies upon recruitment methods of purposive sampling, respondent driven sampling, and snowball sampling.

NextGen. The Next Generation Air Transport System, where satellite-based systems will replace ground-based systems for air traffic management (Curtis, Jentsch, & Wise, 2010).

Obsessive passion. Obsessive passion stems from the need for social acceptance and self-esteem, where the individual's identity becomes the driving force for the passion, more so than the enjoyment (Kocjan, 2015).

Purposive sampling. "A type of nonprobability sampling in which the units to be observed are selected on the basis of researcher's judgment about which ones will be the most useful or representative" (Babbie, 2013, p. 128).

Recency training. A recency event is a simulator training event where a pilot performs three takeoffs and landings, within 90-days, to maintain currency per Federal Aviation Regulation (FAR) 121.439 (GPO, 2015).

Recreational flight. A pilot flies an aircraft on their days off, not for hire, but for enjoyment.

Recurrent simulator training. Recurrent simulator training is an FAA mandate where pilots will receive an approved number of simulator days, per airline, for training and evaluation, conducted on either a sixth month, nine month, or annual cycle (GPO). A typical example for a cycle could be every nine months the pilot will spend two, four-hour sessions in the simulator (day-one and day-two). The first day is training, the second day is checking.

Reserve system. An airline operating system where pilots are paid to standby, on call, in the event they are needed to fly.

Respondent driven sampling. Respondent-driven sampling (RDS), combines "snowball sampling" (getting individuals to refer those they know, these individuals in turn refer those they know and so on) with a mathematical model that weights the sample to compensate for the fact that the sample was collected in a non-random way (Volz, et al., 2012).

Reporting culture. A culture where reporting safety related information is both encouraged and rewarded (Stolzer & Goglia, 2015).

Safety culture. "The shared values, action, and behaviors that demonstrate a commitment to safety over competing goals and demands" (FAA, 2013b, p. 9). A positive safety culture includes five subcultures—reporting culture, a just culture, a flexible culture, an informed culture, and learning culture (Stolzer & Goglia, 2015).

Safety management systems (SMS). "SMS is the formal, top-down, organization-wide approach to managing safety risk and assuring the effectiveness of safety risk controls. It includes systematic procedures, practices, and policies for the management of safety risk" (FAA, 2016, A-2).

Situation awareness. "The perception of the elements in the environment within a volume of time and space, the comprehension of their meaning, and the projection of their status in the near future" (Endsley, 2001, p. 5).

Snowball sampling. Snowball sampling is "a technique for finding research subjects. One subject gives the researcher the name of another subject, who in turn provides the name of a third, and so on" (Atkinson & Flint, as cited in Baltar & Brunet, 2012, p. 60).

Social networking site. A social networking site (SNS) is a "web-based service that allow individuals to construct a public or semi-public profile within a bounded system, articulate a list of other users with whom they share a connection, and view and traverse their list of connections and those made by others within the system" (Boyd & Ellison, as cited in Baltar & Brunet, 2012, p. 58).

Stall. "Aerodynamic loss of lift caused by exceeding the critical angle of attack" (GPO, 2010, p. 2361).

Standard operating procedures. Airline specific operating procedures, that ensure all pilots will perform the same processes and procedures in the flightdeck.

Startle Factor. An unexpected event resulting in an unconscious response (Casner, Geven, & Williams, 2013; Landman, Groen, Van Paassen, Bronkhorst, & Mulder, 2017).

Stick pusher. "A device that, at or near a stall, applies a nose down pitch force to an aircraft's control columns to attempt to decrease the aircraft's angle of attack" (GPO, 2010, p. 2361).

Systematic reflection. "A learning procedure during which learners comprehensively analyze their behavior and evaluate the contribution of its components to performance outcomes" (Ellis, Carette, Anseel & Lievens, 2014, p. 68).

Tactical autoflight. Tactical autoflight indicates that both the autopilot and auto thrust are engaged, but the aircraft is pilot managed with heading, speed, and altitude interventions (FAA, 2016; OIG, 2016).

Targeted sampling. "Targeted sampling includes an initial ethnographic assessment in order to identify the networks that might exist in a given population" (Baltar & Brunet, 2012, p. 60).

Terminal Proficiency Objective (TPO). "TPOs are statements of performance, conditions, and standards established at the task level," written as AQP directives of training (FAA, 2017a, p. 17).

Unconsciously competent. "Unconsciously competent occurs with overlearning in that the knowledge or skill is applied without conscious thought" (Besco, 1997, p. 60).

Unconsciously incompetent. "The crew is unaware that they do not know something or that they cannot do something. In other words, the crew doesn't know what they don't know" (Besco, 1997, p. 58).

Understanding. Understanding is a pilot's ability, beyond knowledge-based facts and memorized procedures, to know why procedures are accomplished, and to identify and understand instrument display indications, enabling the pilot to manage the aircraft during full automation usage (Level 4), or no automation usage (Level 0), whether the automation was intentionally disengaged, or a component failed, within any given environment.

Acronyms

Aviation acronyms—the result of pilots'
inability to spell... or the cause?

AIC	Automation-induced complacency
ADM	Aeronautical Decision Making
AFC	Automated Flight Control
AGFI	Adjusted Goodness of Fit Index
ALPA	Airline Pilots Association
AP	Autopilot
AQP	Advanced Qualification Program
ASAP	Aviation Safety Action Program
ASRS	Aviation Safety Reporting System
AT	Autothrust
ATP	Airline Transport Pilot Certificate
AVE	Average Variance Extracted
BEA	Bureau of Economic Analysis
CA	Captain
CFA	Confirmatory Factor Analysis
CFI	Comparative Fit Index
CMIN/df	Minimum Discrepancy/Degrees of Freedom
CR	Construct Reliability
CRM	Crew Resource Management
CLT	Cognitive Load Theory
EFA	Exploratory Factor Analysis
EICAS	Engine Indication and Crew Alerting System
ESSAI	Enhanced Safety through Situation Awareness Integration in Training
FAA	Federal Aviation Administration
FAR	Federal Aviation Regulation
FD	Flight Director
FMA	Flight Mode Annunciator
FMC	Flight Management Computer
FMS	Flight Management System
FO	First Officer
FOQA	Flight Operational Quality Assurance
GFI	Goodness of Fit Index
GPO	Government Publishing Office
IRB	Institutional Review Board
LCSA	Line Check Safety Audit
LOE	Line Operational Evaluation

LOFT	Line Oriented Flight Training
LOSA	Line Operation Safety Audit
MFI	Manual Flight Inventory
MSA	Measure of Sampling Adequacy
NextGen	Next Generation Air Transport System
NFI	Normal Fit Index
NSTB	National Safety Transportation Board
OIG	Office of Inspector General
PF	Pilot Flying
PM	Pilot Monitoring
RMSEA	Root Mean Square Error
SA	Situation Awareness
SNS	Social Networking System
WG	Working Group

REFERENCES

1. Aaker, J. L., Brumbaugh, A. M., & Grier, S. A. (2000). Nontarget markets and viewer distinctiveness: The impact of target marketing on advertising attitudes. *Journal of Consumer Psychology*, 9(3), 127-140. doi:10.1207/15327660051044105

2. Abbott, K. (2015, November 3). Managing Automation or Managing Aircraft Flight Path: How Does Operational Policy Need to Evolve? *68th Annual International Air Safety Summit*, Miami, FL.

3. Abdi, H. (2003). *Encyclopedia of social sciences research methods.* Thousand Oaks, CA: Sage Publishing

4. Adamski, A. J., & Doyle, T. J. (2005). *Introduction to the aviation regulatory process.* (5th ed.) Plymouth, MI: Hayden-McNeil Publishing, Inc.

5. Air Transport Association's Data Management Focus Group (1998). *Advance qualification data management guide.*

6. Airbus. (2003). Aircraft Operating Manual Volume II. Airbus Industries. France

7. Airbus. (2007). Flight operations briefing notes. *Human performance enhancing situation awareness.*

8. Aldana, K. (2013, May 30). U.S. department of transportation releases policy on automated vehicle development. NHTSA.

9. Anderson, R. (2015, November 3). Keynote. CEO Delta Airlines. *68th Annual International Air Safety Summit*, Miami, FL.

10. Astakhova, M. N. (2015). The curvilinear relationship between work passion and organizational citizenship behavior. *Journal of Business Ethics*, 130(2), 361-374. doi:10.1007/s10551-014-2233-5

11. Atkinson, R., ATKINSON, R., & FLINT, J. (2003). Sampling, snowball: accessing hidden and hard-to-reach populations. In R. L. Miller, & J. D. Brewer, *The A-Z of Social Research. London*, UK: Sage UK.

12. Babbie, E. R. (2013). *The practice of social research*. Belmont, Calif: Wadsworth Cengage.

13. Bailey, N. R., & Scerbo, M. W. (2007). Automation-induced complacency for monitoring highly reliable systems: The role of task complexity, system experience, and operator trust. *Theoretical Issues in Ergonomics Science*, 8(4), 321-348. doi: 10.1080/14639220500535301

14. Baltar, F., & Brunet, I. (2012). Social research 2.0: Virtual snowball sampling method using facebook. *Internet Research*, 22(1), 57-74.

15. Banbury, S., Dudfield, H., Hormann, H., & Soll, H. (2007). FASA: development and validation of a novel measure to assess the effectiveness of commercial airline pilot situation awareness training. *The International Journal of Aviation Psychology*, 17(2), 131-152. doi: 10.1080/10508410701328557.

16. Bandura, A. (1982). Self-efficacy mechanism in human agency. *American Psychologist*, 37(2), 122-147. doi:10.1037/0003-066X.37.2.122

17. Baron, R. M., & Kenny, D. A. (1986). The moderator-mediator variable distinction in social psychological research: Conceptual, strategic and statistical considerations. *Journal of Personality and Social Psychology*, 51, 1173-1182.

18. Barton, E., Eggly, S., Winckles, A., & Albrecht, T. L. (2014). Strategies of persuasion in offers to participate in cancer clinical trials I: Topic placement and topic framing. Communication & Medicine, 11(1), 1-14. doi:10.1558/cam.v11i1.16614

19. *BEA*. (2012, June 1). Flight 447 final report.

20. Bénabou, R., & Tirole, J. (2002). Self-confidence and personal motivation. *The Quarterly Journal of Economics*, 117(3), 871-915. doi:10.1162/003355302760193913

21. Bent, J., & Chan, K. (2010). Flight training and simulation as safety generators. In Salas, E. & Maurino, D. (Eds.) *Human factors in aviation* (2nd ed.). (pp. 293-333).

22. Bentler, P.M. (2001). *EQS 6 structural equations program manual.* Encino, CA: Multivariate Software.

23. Besco, R. O. (1997). Analyzing knowledge deficiencies in pilot performance. *The International Journal of Aviation Psychology*, (2)1, 53-74, doi: 10.1207/s15327108ijap0201_4

24. Besco, R. O. (2004). Human performance breakdowns are rarely accidents: they are usually very poor choices with disastrous results. *Journal of Hazardous Material*, (115)1, 155-161.

25. Bohle Carbonell, K., Stalmeijer, R. E. W., Konings, K. D., Segers, M. S. R., & van Merrienboer, J. J. G. (2014). How experts deal with novel situations: A review of adaptive expertise, *Educational Research Review*, 12, 14-29. Doi: 10.1016/j.edurev.2014.03.001

26. Brown, D. P. (2013, July 19). What is an Avgeek? I am an #avgeek & hear me roar! *Airline Reporter*.

27. Brown, T.A., & Moore, M.T. (2013). Confirmatory factor analysis. In R.H. Hoyle (Ed.), *Handbook of structural equation modeling* (pp. 361-379). New York: Guilford Press.

28. Burt, R. D., PhD, Hagan, H., PhD, Sabin, K., PhD, & Thiede, Hanne, DVM, MPH. (2010). Evaluating respondent-driven sampling in a major metropolitan area: Comparing injection drug users in the 2005 Seattle area national HIV behavioral surveillance system survey with participants in the RAVEN and kiwi studies. *Annals of Epidemiology*, 20(2), 159-167. doi:10.1016/j.annepidem.2009.10.002

29. Byrne, B.M. (2010). *Structural equation modeling with AMOS* (2nd Edition). Routledge, UK; 2010. ISBN 978-0-8058-6372-7.

30. Byrne, B.M. (2010). *Structural Equation Modeling with LISREL.* Mahway, NJ: Lawrence Erlbaum Associates.

31. Casner, S. M., Geven, R. W., & Williams, K. T. (2013). The effectiveness of airline pilot training for abnormal events. *Human Factors*, 55, 477-485. doi:10.1177/0018720812466893.

32. Casner, S. M., & Schooler, J. W. (2014). Thoughts in flight: automation use and pilots' task-related and task-unrelated thought. *Human Factors: The Journal of Human Factors and Ergonomics Society*, 56(3), 433-442. doi:10.1177/0018720813501550

33. Casner, S. M., Geven, R. W., Recker, M. P., & Schooler, J. W. (2014). The retention of manual flying skills in the automated cockpit. *Human Factors* 56, 433-442. doi: 10.1177/0018720813501550.

34. Chakravarti, Laha, and Roy, (1967) *Handbook of Methods of Applied Statistics*, Volume I, John Wiley and Sons, pp. 392-394.

35. Chapman, C., Lane, A., M., Brierley J., H, & Terry P., C. (1997). Anxiety, self-confidence and performance in tae kwon-do. *Perceptual and Motor Skills*. 85,(3), 1275-1278.

36. Chen, C. F., & Chen S.C. (2012). Scale development of safety management system evaluation for the airline industry. *Accident Analysis and Prevention*, 47, 177-181. doi: 10.1016/j.aap.2012.01.012

37. Civic Impulse. (2016). H.R. 3371 — *111th Congress: Airline Safety and Pilot Training Improvement Act of 2009.*

38. Cohen, J. (1988) *Statistical Power Analysis for the Behavioral Sciences.* (2nd Ed.). Lawrence Earlbaum Associates, Mahway, NJ.

39. Cohen, J., Cohen, P., West, S. G., & Aiken, L. S. (2003). *Applied multiple regression/correlation analysis for the behavioral sciences.* (3rd ed.). Mahwah, NJ: Lawrence Erlbaum Associates.

40. Collins, J. (2001). *Why some companies make the leap and others don't. Good to great.* New York, NY. HarperCollins.

41. Compte, O., & Postlewaite, A. (2004). Confidence-enhanced performance. *The American Economic Review*, 94(5), 1536-1557. doi:10.1257/0002828043052204

42. Connell, L. (2012, June 18). ASRS Marks 1 Million Anonymous Reports, *National Business Aviation Association.*

43. Confusion. (n.d.). In *Merriam-Webster's online dictionary* (11th ed.).

44. Conti, G. J. (2009). Development of a user-friendly instrument for identifying the learning strategy preferences of adults. *Teaching and Teacher Education*, 25(6), 887-896. doi:10.1016/j.tate.2009.02.024

45. Costello, A. B. and Osborne, J. W. (2005). Best practices in exploratory factor analysis: four recommendations for getting the most from your analysis. *Practical Assessment Research & Evaluation*, 10(7).

46. Cuevas, H. M. (2003). The pilot personality and individual differences in the stress response. *Proceedings of the Human Factors and Ergonomics Society 47th Annual Meeting* (pp. 1092-1096). Santa Monica, CA: Human Factors and Ergonomics Society.

47. Curry, R. E. (1985). The introduction of new cockpit technology: a human factors study. *NASA Technical Report Server*.

48. Curtis, M., T., Jentsch, F., & Wise, J. A. (2010). Aviation displays. In Salas, E. & Maurino, D. (Eds.) *Human factors in aviation* (2nd ed.). (pp. 439-476). Burlington, MA: Academic Press—Elsevier.

49. Dahlstrom, N., Dekker, S., Van Winsen, R., & Nycy, J. (2008). Fidelity and validity of simulator training. *Theoretical Issues in Ergonomics* Science, 10 (4) 305-314. doi:10.1080/14639220802368864.

50. Darr, S., Ricks, W., & Lemos, K. (2010, June). Safer systems: A NextGen aviation strategic goal. *IEEE Aerospace & Electronics Systems Magazine*, 25(6), 9-14.

51. DataUSA. (2018a). *Line Pilot of Age by Gender for Aircraft Pilots*. [Chart].

52. DataUSA. (2018b). *Line Pilot of Age by Gender for Aircraft Pilots Demographics*. [Table].

53. Davidson, J. (2015, May 26). Here's how many internet users there are. *Money*.

54. Degani, A., Barshi, I., & Shafto, M. G. (2013). Information organization in the airline cockpit: lessons from flight 236. *Journal of Cognitive Engineering and Decision Making*, 7, 330-352. doi:10.1177/155343413492983.

55. De Winter, C.F. and Dodou, D. (2011). Common factor analysis versus principal component analysis: a comparison of loadings by means of simulations. *Journal of communications in Statistics- Simulation and Computation*. 45(1), 299-321. doi.org/10.1080/03610918.2013.862274.

56. Dillman, D. A., Smyth, J. D., & Christian, L. M. (2009). *Internet, mail, and mixed-mode surveys: The tailored design method* (Third ed.). Hoboken, N.J: Wiley & Sons.

57. Dismukes, R., K. (2010). Understanding an analyzing human error in real-world operations. In Salas, E. & Maurino, D. (Eds.) *Human factors in aviation* (2nd ed.). (pp. 335-374). Burlington, MA: Academic Press—Elsevier.

58. Dismukes, R. K., Berman, B. A., & Loukopoulos, L. D. (2007). *The limits of expertise: rethinking pilot error and the causes of airline accidents*. Burlington, VT: Ashgate Publishing Co.

59. Dubicki, E. (2007). Basic marketing and promotion concepts. *The Serials Librarian*, 53(3), 5-15. doi:10.1300/J123v53n03_02

60. Dziubaniuk, O. (2014). Trust in online marketing: Trustful business relationship building by search engine marketers. *Business & Professional Ethics Journal*, 33(4), 1.

61. Ellis, S., Carette, B., Anseel, F., & Lievens, F. (2014). Systematic reflection: implications for learning from failures and successes. *Current Directions in Psychological Science* (23)1 67-72. doi: 10.1177/0963721413504106

62. Endsley, M. R. (1995). Toward a theory of situation awareness in dynamic systems. *Human Factors*, 37(1), 32-64. doi: 10.1518/001872095779049543.

63. Endsley, M. R. (2001). Training for situation awareness. *Presentation to the Royal Aeronautical Society* (pp. 1-16).

64. Endsley, M. R. (2010). Situation Awareness in Aviation Systems. In J. A. Wise, V. D. Hopkin, & D. J. Garland (Eds.), *Handbook of aviation human factors* (2nd ed.) (pp. 12-1 - 12-18). Boca Raton, FL: CRC Press – Taylor & Francis.

65. Endsley, M. R. and Garland, D. J. (2000) Situation Awareness Analysis and Measurement. Mahwah, NJ: Lawrence Erlbaum Associates

66. Endsley, M. R. & Jones, D. G. (2012). *Designing for situation awareness an approach to user-centered design.* (2nd ed.). Boca Raton, FL. Taylor & Francis Group.

67. English, M. C. W., & Visser, T. A. W. (2014). Exploring the repetition paradox: The effects of learning context and massed repetition on memory. *Psychonomic Bulletin & Review*, 21(4), 1026-1032.

68. Ericsson, A. K. (2008). Deliberate practice and acquisition of expert performance: A general overview. *Academic Emergency Medicine*, 15(11), 988-994. doi:10.1111/j.1553-2712.2008.00227.x

69. Esser, D., A. (2005). *Advanced qualification program training in threat and error mitigation: an analysis of the use of line check safety audits for validation.* (Doctoral dissertation, Capella University).

70. FAA. (1991). *Aeronautical Decision Making* (Advisory Circular AC 60-22). US Department of Transportation, Washington, DC.

71. FAA. (1996, June 18). *The interfaces between flightcrews and modern flight deck systems.* Human factors team report.

72. FAA. (2004a). *Flight Operations Quality Assurance* (Advisory Circular AC 120-82). US Department of Transportation, Washington, DC.

73. FAA. (2004b). Line operational simulations: line oriented flight training, special purpose operational training, line operational evaluation.

74. (Advisory Circular AC 120-35c). US Department of Transportation, Washington, DC.

75. FAA. (2008, June 13). *Extended operations (ETOPS) and operations in the north polar area.* (Advisory Circular. AC 120-42b).

76. FAA. (2013a, January 4). *Safety alert for operators: manual flight operations.* SAFO Publication No.13002.

77. FAA. (2013b, April 11). *Safety management system* 8000.369A.

78. FAA. (2013c, July 10). *Press release – FAA boosts aviation safety with new pilot qualification standards.*

79. FAA. (2013d, September 5). *Operational use of flight path management systems: final report of the performance-based operations.* Aviation Rule Making Committee / Commercial Aviation Safety Team Flight Deck Automation Working Group.

80. FAA. (2015a, January 7). *Rule advances U.S. airline industry's proactive safety culture*. Press Release—FAA final rule requires safety management system for airlines.

81. FAA. (2015b). *Safety Management Systems for Aviation Service Providers*. (Advisory Circular 120-92B).

82. FAA. (2015c, August 5). *Air Transat Flight TSC236, A330 Location: Terceira Airport, Azores*.

83. FAA. (2015d, October 5). *Reduced vertical separation minimum* (RVSM).

84. FAA. (2016, March 3). Order 8000.369B. SUBJ Safety Management Systems. U.S. Department of Transportation Federal Aviation Administration.

85. FAA. (2016, August 19). *NextGen*.

86. FAA. (2017a). *Advanced qualification program*. (Advisory Circular AC 120-54A). US Department of Transportation, Washington, DC.

87. FAA. (2017b, February 01). U.S. civil airman statistics.

88. Fabrigar, L. R., Wegener, D. T., MacCallum, R. C., & Strahan, E. J. (1999). Evaluating the use of exploratory factor analysis in psychological research. *Psychological Methods*, 4(3), 272-299.

89. Ferris, T., Sarter, N., & Wickens, C. D. (2010). Cockpit automation: still struggling to catch up. In Salas, E. & Maurino, D. (Eds.) *Human factors in aviation* (2nd ed.). (pp. 479-503).

90. Field, A. (2013). Discovering Statistics Using SPSS (3rd Edition). Thousand Oaks, CA: Sage Publications Ltd.

91. Fischer, I., & Budescu, D., V. (2005). When do those who know more also know more about how much they know? The development of confidence and performance in categorical decision tasks. *Organizational Behavior and Human Decision Processes*, (98)1, 39-53. doi:10.1016/j.obhdp.2005.04.003

92. Flora, D. B., & Flake, J. K. (2017). The Purpose and Practice of Exploratory and Confirmatory Factor Analysis in Psychological Research: Decisions for Scale Development and Validation. *Canadian Journal of Behavioural Science*. (49) 2. 78-88.

93. Fraher, A. L. (2015, July 21). Technology–push, market-demand and the missing safety-pull: a case study of American Airlines Flight 587. *New Technology, Work and Employment*, 30(2),109-127. doi: 10.1111/ntwe.12050

94. Franks, P., Hay, H., & Mavin, T. (2014). Can competency-based training fly?: an overview of key issues for ab initio pilot training. *International Journal of Training Research*, 12(2), 132-147.

95. Funk, K., Lyall, B., Wilson, J., Vint, R., Niemczyk, M., Suroteguh, C., & Owen, G. (1999). Flight deck automation issues. The International Journal of Aviation Psychology, 9(2), 109-123.

96. Gain (2004). A roadmap to a just culture: Enhancing the safety environment.

97.   Gao, Y., Bruce, P. J., Newman, D. G., & Zhang, C. B. (2013). Safety climate of commercial pilots: The effect of pilot ranks and employment experiences. *Journal of Air Transport Management, 30,* 17-24. doi:10.1016/j.jairtraman.2013.04.001

98.   Garson, David (2012). *Testing statistical assumptions* (2nd ed.). Asheboro, NC: Statistical Associates Publishing.

99.   Gaskin, J. (2017a, March 28). *StatWiki.*

100. Gaskin, J. (2017b, September 22). *StatWiki.*

101. Gesell, L. E., & Dempsey, P.S. (2011). *Aviation and the law.* (5th ed.). Chandler, AZ: Coast Aire Publications.

102. Geiselman, E. E., Johnson, C. M., & Buck, D. R. (2013). Flight deck automation: invaluable collaborator or insidious enabler? *Ergonomics in Design: The Quarterly of Human Factors Applications, 2,* 22-26.

103. Giles, C. N. (2013). Modern airline pilots' quandary: Standard operating procedures-to comply or not to comply. *Journal of Aviation Technology and Engineering, 2*(2), 1. doi:10.7771/2159-6670.1070

104. Gluck, K. (2010). Cognitive architectures for human factors in aviation. In Salas, E. & Maurino, D. (Eds.) *Human factors in aviation* (2nd ed.). (pp. 375-399). Burlington, MA: Academic Press—Elsevier.

105. Goh, S. C. (2003). Improving organizational learning capability: Lessons from two case studies. *The Learning Organization, 10*(4), 216-227. doi:10.1108/09696470310476981

106. Gonzalez, C., Best, B., Healy, A. F., Kole, J. A., Bourne Jr. L. E. (2011). A cognitive modeling account of simultaneous learning and fatigue effects. *Cognitive Systems Research, 12*(1) 19-32

107. Gorsuch, R. L. (1983). *Factor analysis* (2nd Associates.ed.). Hillsdale, NJ: Lawrence Erlbaum.

108. GPO. (2010, August 01). Airline safety and federal aviation administration extension act of 2010. Public law 11-216.

109. GPO. (2015, May 28). Electronic code of federal regulations.

110. Grieve, R., Witteveen, K., & Tolan, G. A. (2014). Social media as a tool for data collection: Examining equivalence of socially value-laden constructs. *Current Psychology, 33*(4), 532-544. doi:10.1007/s12144-014-9227-4

111. Grant-Muller, S. M., Gal-Tzur, A., Minkov, E., Nocera, S., Kuflik, T., & Shoor, I. (2015;2014;). Enhancing transport data collection through social media sources: Methods, challenges and opportunities for textual data. *IET Intelligent Transport Systems, 9*(4), 407-417. doi:10.1049/iet-its.2013.0214

112. Groves, R. M., Presser, S., & Dipko, S. (2004). The role of topic interest in survey participation decisions. *The Public Opinion Quarterly, 68*(1), 2-31. doi:10.1093/poq/nfh002

113. Hair, J. F., Black, W. C., Babin, B. J., & Anderson, R. E. (2006). *Multivariate data analysis* (6th ed.). Upper Saddle River, NJ: Prentice Hall.

114. Hair, J.F., Black, W.C., Babin, B.J., and Anderson, R.E. (2010). *Multivariate Data Analysis*. 7th Edition, Upper Saddle River, NJ: Pearson Prentice Hall.

115. Harris, D. (2012). The human factors that relate to technological developments in aviation. In Young, T., M., & Hirst, M. (Eds.) *Innovation in aeronautics* (pp. 132-154). Philadelphia: Woodhead Publishing.

116. Haslbeck, A., Ekkehart, S., Onnasch, L., Huttig, G., Bubb, H., & Bengler, K. (2012). Manual flying skills under the influence of performance shaping factors. *IOS Press*, 41 178-183. doi:10.3233/WOR-2012-0153-178.

117. Haslbeck, A., & Hoermann, H. (2016). Flying the needles: Flight deck automation erodes fine-motor flying skills among airline pilots. *Human Factors*, 58(4), 533. doi:10.1177/0018720816640394

118. Hattie, J., & Timperley, H. (2007). The power of feedback. *Review of Educational Research*, 77(1), 81–112. doi:10.3102/003465430298487

119. Heckathorn, D. (1997). Respondent-Driven Sampling: A New Approach to the Study of Hidden Populations. *Social Problems*, 44(2), 174-199. doi:10.2307/3096941

120. Helmreich, R. L., Merritt, A.C., & Wilhelm, J.A. (1999). The evolution of crew resource management training in commercial aviation. *International Journal of Aviation Psychology* 9(1), 19-32.

121. Helmreich, R. L. (2000). On error management: Lessons from aviation. *BMJ: British Medical Journal*, 320(7237), 781-785. doi:10.1136/bmj.320.7237.781

122. Helmreich, R.L. & Klinect, J.R. & Wilhelm, J.A.. (2001). System safety and threat and error management: The line operations safety audit (LOSA). *Proceedings of the Eleventh International Symposium on Aviation Psychology*. 1-6.

123. Hendrickson, S. M. L., Goldsmith, T. E., & Johnson, P. J. (2006). Retention of airline pilots knowledge and skill. *Human Factors and Ergonomics Society Annual Meeting Proceedings*, 50(17), 1973-1976.

124. Hertzog, M. A. (2008). Considerations in determining sample size for pilot studies. *Research in Nursing & Health*, 31(2), 180-191. doi:10.1002/nur.20247

125. Ho, V. T., Wong, S., & Lee, C. H. (2011). A tale of passion: Linking job passion and cognitive engagement to employee work performance. *Journal of Management Studies*, 48(1), 26-47. doi:10.1111/j.1467-6486.2009.00878.x

126. Hu, L. & Bentler, P. (1999). Fit Indices in Covariance Structure Modeling: Sensitivity to Underparameterized Model Misspecification. *Psychological Methods* (1999), 3(4) 424-453.

127. Huddleston, H., F., & Rolfe, J., M. (1971). Behavioural factors influencing the use of flight simulators for training. *Applied Ergonomics*, 2(3) 141-148.

128. Huhtala, M., Tolvanen, A., Mauno, S., & Feldt, T. (2015). The associations between ethical organizational culture, burnout, and engagement: A multilevel study. *Journal of Business and Psychology*, 30(2), 399-414. doi:10.1007/s10869-014-9369-2

129. Hurley, A. E., Scandura, T. A., Schriesheim, C. A., & Brannick, M. T. (1997). Exploratory and confirmatory factor analysis: Guidelines, issues, and alternatives: Introduction. Journal of Organizational Behavior (1986-1998), 18(6), 667.

130. ICAO (2014) *Manual of aeroplane upset prevention and recovery training.* (Doc 10011 AN/506)

131. Jackman, F. (2012). Startle effect. *Flight Safety Foundation.*

132. Jamieson, G. A., & Vicente, K. J. (2005). Designing effective human-automation-plant interfaces: A control-theoretic perspective. *Human Factors: The Journal of the Human Factors and Ergonomics Society*, 47(1), 12-34. doi:10.1518/0018720053653820

133. Jipp, M., & Ackerman, P. L. (2016). The impact of higher levels of automation on performance and situation awareness: A function of information-processing ability and working-memory capacity. *Journal of Cognitive Engineering and Decision Making*, 10(2), 138-166. doi:10.1177/1555343416637517

134. Johnson, D. P., & Fowler, J. H. (2011). The evolution of overconfidence. *Nature*, 477(7364), 317-320. doi:10.1518/001872095779049543.

135. Johnson, P., J., & Goldsmith, T., G. (2016, September, 10). The *Importance* of *Quality Data in Evaluating Aircrew Performance.*

136. Kaber, D., B., & Endsley, M., R. (2004). The effects of level of automation and adaptive automation on human performance, situation awareness, and workload in a dynamic control task. *Theoretical issues in Ergonomics Science*, (5)2 113-153. doi: 10.1080/1463922021000054335

137. Kahan, D., & Al-tamimi, A. (2009). Strategies for recruiting middle eastern-american young adults for physical activity research: A case of snowballs and salaam. *Journal of Immigrant and Minority Health*, 11(5), 380-90. doi:http://dx.doi.org.ezproxy.libproxy.db.erau.edu/10.1007/s10903-008-9117-7

138. Kaiser H.F. (1960). The application of electronic computers to factor analysis. *Educational and Psychological Measurement*. 20:141-51. doi. org/10.1177/001316446002000116

139. Kalyuga, S. (2009). Knowledge elaboration: A cognitive load perspective. *Learning and Instruction*, 19(5), 402-410.

140. Kass, R. E., & Wasserman, L. (1995). A reference bayesian test for nested hypotheses and its relationship to the schwarz criterion. *Journal of the American Statistical Association*, 90(431), 928-934. doi:10.1080/0162 1459.1995.10476592

141. Ke, T. (2001). Minimum sample sizes for conducting exploratory factor analyses (Order No. 3006596). Available from ProQuest Dissertations & Theses Global. (276265637).

142. Kenny DA, Bolger N, Korchmaros JD. 2003. Lower-level mediation in multilevel models. Psychol. Methods 8:115–28

143. Kern, T. (1998). *Flight discipline.* McGraw Hill.

144. King, D. B., O'Rourke, N., & DeLongis, A. (2014). Social media recruitment and online data collection: A beginner's guide and best practices for accessing low-prevalence and hard-to-reach populations. *Canadian Psychology/Psychologie Canadienne,* 55(4), 240-249. doi:10.1037/a0038087

145. Khine, M.S. (2013). Application of Structural Equation Modeling in Educational Research and Practice. Sense Publishers. AW Rotterdam, Netherlands.

146. Kline, R., B. (2011). *Principles and practice of structural equation modeling.* (3rd ed.). New York, NY: Gilford Press.

147. Kline, P. (1994). *An easy guide to factor analysis.* London; New York: Routledge.

148. Knowles, M. S., Swanson, R. A., Holton, E.,F., & Ellwood, F. (2011). *The adult learner: The definitive classic in adult education and human resource development* (7th ed.). Kidlington, Oxford; Burlington, MA; Routledge.

149. Kocjan, G. Z. (2015). Disentangling the overlap between employee engagement and passion. *Psychological Topics,* 24(2), 233.

150. Kole, J. A., Healy, A. F., Fierman, D. M., & Bourne, L. E. (2010). Contextual memory and skill transfer in category search. *Memory & Cognition* 38(1) pp. 67-82

151. Kossman, N. A. (2016). *How work factors contribute to engagement, passion, motivation, and performance in entertainment* (Order No. 10126651). Available from ProQuest Dissertations & Theses Global. (1808906182).

152. Krois, P., Piccione, D., & McCloy, T. (2010). Commentary on NextGen and aviation human factors. In E. Salas & D. Maurino (Eds.), *Human factors in aviation* (2nd ed.) (pp. 701-708). Burlington, MA: Academic Press – Elsevier.

153. Landman, A., Groen, E. L., Van Paassen, M. M., Bronkhorst, A. W., & Mulder, M. (2017). Dealing with unexpected events on the flight deck: A conceptual model of startle and surprise. *Human Factors: The Journal of Human Factors and Ergonomics Society,* 59(8), 1161-1172. doi:10.1177/0018720817723428

154. Lavrakas, P. J. (Ed.). (2008). *Encyclopedia of survey research methods.* Thousand Oaks, CA: SAGE Publications Ltd. doi: 10.4135/9781412963947

155. Lee, Y., & Trim, P. R. J. (2006). Retail marketing strategy: The role of marketing intelligence, relationship marketing and trust. *Marketing Intelligence & Planning*, 24(7), 730-745. doi:10.1108/02634500610711888

156. Lelaie, C. (2012, January). A380: Development of the flight controls. *The Airbus Safety magazine*, Safety First, 13, 22-25.

157. Leva, M. C., Cahill, J., Kay, A. M., Losa, G., & McDonald, N. (2010). The advancement of a new human factors report - 'The Unique Report' – facilitating flight crew auditing of performance/operations as part of an airline's safety management system. *Ergonomics*, 53(2). 164-183. doi: 10.1080/00140130903437131.

158. Lindseth, P. D., Lindseth, G., N., Petros, T. V., Jensen, W. & Caspers, J. (2013). Effects of hydration on cognitive function of pilots. *Military Medicine*, 178(7), 792-8.

159. Liao, M. (2015). Safety culture in commercial aviation: Differences in perspective between chinese and western pilots. *Safety Science*, 79, 193-205. doi:10.1016/j.ssci.2015.05.011

160. Lowy, J. (2011, August 31). Automation in the sky dulls airline-pilot skill. *Daily News*.

161. MacCallum, R. C., Widaman, K. F., Preacher, K. J., & Hong, S. (2001). Sample size in factor analysis: The role of model error. *Multivariate Behavioral Research,* 36(4), 611-637. doi:10.1207/S15327906MBR3604_06

162. MacKenzie, S. B., Podsakoff, P. M., & Podsakoff, N. P. (2011). Construct measurement and validation procedures in MIS and behavioral research: Integrating new and existing techniques. *MIS Quarterly*, 35(2), 293-334.

163. MacKenzie, S. B., & Podsakoff, P. M. (2012). Common method bias in marketing: Causes, mechanisms, and procedural remedies. *Journal of Retailing*, 88(4), 542-555. doi:10.1016/j.jretai.2012.08.001

164. Mager, R. F., & Pipe, P. (1997). *Analyzing performance problems or you really oughta wanna* (3rd ed.). Belmont, CA: Lake Publishers.

165. Makarowski, R., Makarowski, P., Smolicz, T., & Plopa, M. (2016). Risk profiling of airline pilots: Experience, temperamental traits and aggression. *Journal of Air Transport Management*, 57, 298-305. doi:10.1016/j.jairtraman.2016.08.013

166. Malhotra N. K., Dash S. (2011). Marketing Research an Applied Orientation. London: Pearson Publishing.

167. Mathew J. W. & Thomas (2004) Predictors of threat and error management: identification of core nontechnical skills and implications for training systems design, *The International Journal of Aviation Psychology*, 14(2). 207-231, doi: 10.1207/s15327108ijap1402_6

168. Matton, N., Raufaste, E., & Vautier, S. (2013). External validity of individual differences in multiple cue probability learning: the case of pilot training. *Judgment and Decision Making*, (8)5, 589-602.

169. Maurino, D. E. (2000). Human factors and aviation safety: what the industry has, what the industry needs, *Ergonomics* 43(7) 952-959, doi: 10.1080/001401300409134.

170. Mavin, T. J., & Roth, M. (2014a). Between reflection on practice and the practice of reflection: a case study from aviation. *Reflective Practice*, 15(5), 651-665. doi:10.1080/14623943.2014.944125

171. Mavin, T. J., & Roth, W. (2014b). Optimizing a workplace learning pattern: a case study from aviation. *Journal of Workplace Learning*, 27(2), 112-127. doi:10.1108/JWL-07-2014-0055

172. McClumpha, A. J., James, M., Green, R. G., & Belyavin, A. J. (1991). Pilots' attitudes to cockpit automation. *Human Factors and Ergonomics Society Annual Meeting Proceedings* 35(2) 107-111. doi: 10.1518/107118191786755698

173. Mearns, K. J., & Flin, R. (1999). Assessing the state of organizational safety—culture or climate? *Current Psychology: Developmental, Learning, Personality, Social* 18(1) 5-17.

174. Merkt, R. J. (2009). A computational model on surprise and its effects on agent behavior in simulated environment. *Technical Report*. NLR-TP-2009-637. Amsterdam, Netherlands: National Aerospace Laboratory.

175. Moll, N. (2012, May 2). AIN Blog: Shedding light on automation's dark side [Web log post].

176. Naidoo, Pl, & Vermeulen, L. (2014). Validation of the automation attitude questionnaire for airline pilots. *Ergonomics SA*, 26(1), 44.

177. NASA. (2015). ASRS program briefing. *Aviation safety reporting system*, (pp. 1-54).

178. Naidoo, P. & Vermeulen, L. (2014). Validation of the automation attitude questionnaire for airline pilots. *Ergonomics SA* 26(1) 44-63.

179. Nakamura, J., & Csikszentmihalyi, M. (2003). The construction of meaning through vital engagement. *Flourishing: Positive psychology and the life well-lived*, 83-104.

180. Nemeth, L. (2015, November 4). Using safety data to improve training and ultimately safety. *68th Annual International Air Safety Summit*, Miami, FL.

181. NTSB. (1992). Continental Express Flight 2574 in-flight structural breakup. Report number: NTSB/AAR-92/04.

182. NTSB. (1997). In-flight fire and impact with terrain. ValueJet Airlines Flight 592. Report number: NTSB/AAR-97/06

183. NTSB. (2001). In-Flight Separation of Vertical Stabilizer American Airlines Flight 587. Report number: PB2004-910404

184. NTSB. (2009, February 2). Loss of thrust in both engines after encountering a flock of birds and subsequent ditching on the Hudson River US Airways Flight 1549. Report number: NTSB/AAR-10/03 PB2010-910403

185. NTSB. (2010, February 2). Loss of control on approach, Colgan Air, Inc., operating as Continental Connection Fight 3407.

186. NTSB. (2014a, June 24). Descent below visual glidepath and impact with weawall, Asiana Airlines Flight 214.

187. NTSB. (2014b, February 20). UPS Flight 1354 Accident Investigation.

188. NTSB. (2015). ASRS program briefing.

189. Office of the Inspector General. (2016, January 7). *Enhanced FAA oversight could reduce hazards associated with increased use of flight deck automation.* (Report number AV-2016-013).

190. Paas, F., Renkl, A., & Sweller, J. (2004). Cognitive load theory: instructional implications of the interaction between information structures and cognitive architecture. *Instructional Science*, 32(1-2), 1-8. doi:10.1023/B:TRUC.0000021806.17516.d0.

191. Palinkas, L. A., Horwitz, S. M., Green, C. A., Wisdom, J. P., Duan, N., & Hoagwood, K. (2015). Purposeful sampling for qualitative data collection and analysis in mixed method implementation research. *Administration and Policy in Mental Health*, 42(5), 533–544.

192. Palmer, B. (2013). *Understanding Air France 447*. Los Angeles, California: Self published

193. Parasuraman, R., Molloy, R., & Singh, I. (1993). Performance consequences of automation induced complacency. *The International Journal of Aviation Psychology*, 3(1), 1-23.

194. Parasuraman, R., & Riley, V. (1997). Humans and automation: Use, misuse, disuse, abuse. *Human Factors: The Journal of the Human Factors and Ergonomics Society*, 39(2), 230-253. doi:10.1518/001872097778543886

195. Parasuraman, R., & Wickens, C. D. (2008). Humans: Still vital after all these years of automation. Human Factors: *The Journal of the Human Factors and Ergonomics Society*, 50(3), 511-520. doi:10.1518/001872008X312198

196. Park, C. S. (2013). Does twitter motivate involvement in politics? tweeting, opinion leadership, and political engagement. *Computers in Human Behavior*, 29(4), 1641-1648. doi:10.1016/j.chb.2013.01.044

197. Patankar, M. S., & Sabin, E. J., (2010). The safety culture perspective. In Salas, E. & Maurino, D. (Eds.) *Human factors in aviation* (2nd ed.). (pp. 95-122). Burlington, MA: Academic Press—Elsevier.

198. Petitt K. K. (2017). Structural redesign of pilot training and the automated aircraft. *International Journal of Aviation Systems, Operations and Training* (IJASOT), 4(2), 32-44. doi: 10.4018/IJASOT.2017070103

199. Petitt K. K. (2017). SMS, Safety Culture, and the Four Pillars of Safety Applied to Airline Pilot Training: NextGen Demands to Improve Safety. *International Journal of Aviation Systems, Operations and Training* (IJASOT), 4(2), 45-61. doi: 10.4018/IJSOT.2017070103

200. Petitt, K., K., (2015b, July 13). Airline pilots wanted. To take a survey [Blog Post].

201. Petitt, K., K., (2018a, January 25). General aviation on the rise! With flight bag technology [Blog post].

202. Petitt, K., K, (2018b, March 22). ATC & aviation safety. Helping to make a better system! [Blog post].

203. Petitt, K., K., (2018c, May 25). David Streif. Friday's fabulous flyer. [Blog post].

204. Podsakoff, P. M., MacKenzie, S. B., Lee, J.-Y., & Podsakoff, N. P. (2003). Common method biases in behavioral research: A critical review of the literature and recommended remedies. *Journal of Applied Psychology*, 88(5), 879-903

205. Pons, D., & Dey, K. (2015). Aviation human error modeled as a production process. *The Ergonomics Open Journal*. 8(1) 1-12. doi: 10.2174/1875 934301508010001

206. Pub. L. 111-216. Airline Safety and Federal Aviation Administration Extension Act of 2010, 124 stat 2348.

207. Puentes, A. F. (2011). *The manual flight skill of modern airline pilots* (Order No. 1505741). Available from ProQuest Dissertations & Theses Global. (920120523).

208. Query, J. L., Jr., & Wright, K. B. (2003). Assessing communication competence in an on-line study: Toward informing subsequent interventions among older adults with cancer, their lay caregivers, and peers. Health Communication, 15(2), 205–219.

209. Reason, J. (1997). *Managing the risk of organizational accidents*. Aldershot, UK: Ashgate.

210. Reber, R., Ruch-Monachon, M., & Perrig, W. J. (2007). Decomposing intuitive components in a conceptual problem solving task. *Consciousness and Cognition*, 16(2), 294-309. doi:10.1016/j.concog.2006.05.004

211. Rezaei, F., Nedjat, S., Golestan, B., & Majdzadeh, R. (2011). Reasons for smoking among male teenagers in Tehran, Iran: Two case-control studies using snowball sampling. *International Journal of Preventive Medicine*, 2(4), 216-223.

212. Rosay, J. (2003, December). High-altitude manual flying. *The Airbus Safety magazine, Safety First*, 22, 39-52.

213. Ross, G., & Tomko, L., (2016). Confusion in the cockpit: typology, antecedents, and sources. *Proceedings of the Human Factors and Ergonomics Society Annual meeting*. 60(1), 1299-13-3. doi: 10.1177/1541931213601301

214. Rosenthal, L. J., Chamberlin, R. W., & Matchette, R. D. (1993). Confusion on the flight deck. *Paper presented at the Seventh International Symposium on Aviation Psychology*, Dayton, OH.

215. Roth, W. (2015). Flight examiners' methods of ascertaining pilot proficiency. *The International Journal of Aviation Psychology*, 25(3-4), 209. doi: 10.1080/10508414.2015.1162642

216. Roughton, J., & Crutchfeild, N. (2014). Safety culture an innovative leadership approach. Oxford, UK: Elsevier.

217. Ruel, E., Wagner, W. E. III, & Gillespie, B. J. (2016). *The practice of survey research theory and applications*. London, UK: Sage Publications Inc.

218. Salas, E., Maurino, D., Curtis, M., (2010). Human factors in aviation: an overview. In Salas E. & Maurino, D. (Eds.), *Human factors in aviation* (2nd ed.) (pp. 3-17). Burlington, MA: Academic Press – Elsevier.

219. Salganik, M. J., & Heckathorn, D. D. (2004). Sampling and estimation in hidden populations using respondent-driven sampling. *Sociological Methodology*, 34(1), 193-239. doi:10.1111/j.0081-1750.2004.00152.x

220. Sarter, N. B. &Woods, D. D. (1998) Learning from automation surprises and "going sour" accidents: Progress on human-centered automation. *Cognitive Engineering in Aerospace Applications*. NASA AMES research center. NCC-2-592

221. Schaufeli, W. B., Taris, T. W., & van Rhenen, W. (2008). Workaholism, burnout, and work engagement: Three of a kind or three different kinds of employee well-being? *Applied Psychology an International Review*, 57(2), 173-203. doi:10.1111/j.1464-0597.2007.00285.x

222. Schein, E., H., (2010). *Organizational culture and leadership*. (4th ed.) San Francisco, CA: Jossey-Bass.

223. Schumacher, R.E., Lomax, R.G. (2010). *A Beginner's Guide to Structural Equation Modeling*. 3rd edition, New York, NY: Routledge, Taylor & Francis Group.

224. Schutte, P. C., Fitzgibbons, A., & Davis, D. (2004). *Pilot personality profile using the NEO-PI-R.*

225. Scovel III, C., L., (2012). Progress and challenges in responding to key provisions of the airline safety act. *Before the committee on commerce, science, and transportation subcommittee of aviation, United States Senate*. Department of Transportation.

226. Seat Guru (2018, December 15) Browse airlines. Retried from https://www.seatguru.com/browseairlines

227. Sheridan, T., B. (2010). The system perspective on human factors in aviation. In Salas, E. & Maurino, D. (Eds.) *Human factors in aviation* (2nd ed.). (pp. 23-63).

228. Sherman, P. J., Helmreich, R. L., & Merritt, A. C. (1997). National culture and flight deck automation: Results of a multination survey. *The International Journal of Aviation Psychology*, 7(4), 311-329. doi:10.1207/s15327108ijap0704_4

229. Sibona, C., & Walczak, S. (2012). Purposive sampling on Twitter: A case study. Paper presented at the 3510-3519. doi:10.1109/HICSS.2012.493

230. Sitzmann, T., Ely, K., Brown, K. G., & Bauer, K. N. (2010). Self-assessment of knowledge: A cognitive learning or affective measure? *Academy of Management Learning & Education*, 9(2), 169-191. doi:10.5465/AMLE.2010.51428542

231. Skitka, L., Mosier, K. L., Burdick M., & Rosenblatt, B. (2000). Automation bias and errors: are crews better than individuals? *The International Journal of Aviation Psychology*, 10(1) 85-97, doi: 10.1207/S15327108IJAP1001_5

232. Smith, E. M., Ford, J. K., & Kozlowski, S. W. J. (1997). Building adaptive expertise: Implications for training design strategies. In M. A. Quinones & A. Ehrenstein (Eds.), Training for a rapidly changing workplace: Applications of psychological research (pp. 89-118). Washington, D. C.: American Psychological Association.

233. Snowball sample. (2006). In N. Abercrombie, S. Hill, & B. S. Turner, *The Penguin dictionary of sociology* (5th ed.). London, UK: Penguin.

234. Soper, D. (2017a, March 25). Formulas: A-priori Sample Size or Structural Equation Models.

235. Soper, D. (2017b, March 25). A-priori Sample Size Calculator for Structural Equation Models.

236. Spence, P. R., Lachlan, K. A., & Rainear, A. M. (2016). Social media and crisis research: Data collection and directions. *Computers in Human Behavior*, 54, 667-672. doi:10.1016/j.chb.2015.08.045

237. Statistics Solutions. (2013). Normality [WWW Document].

238. Stewart, I. I., & John, E. (2006). Locus of Control, Attribution Theory, and the" Five Deadly Sins" of Aviation (No. ARI-TR-1182). Army Research Inst For The Behavioral And Social Sciences Fort Rucker Al Rotary-Wing Aviation Research Unit.

239. Stolzer, A. J., Halford, C. D., & Goglia, J. J. (2011). *Implementing safety management systems in aviation*. Burlington, VT: Ashgate.

240. Stolzer, A. J., & Goglia, J. J. (2015). *Safety management systems in aviation*. Burlington, VT: Ashgate.

241. Strauch, B., (2016). The automation-by expertise-by-training Interaction: why automation-related accidents continue to occur in sociotechnical system. *Human Factors: The Journal of the Human Factors and Ergonomics Society. 1-25* doi: 10.1177/0018720816665459

242. Stromberg, R. (2016). The last black sheep. The story of Ed Harper man who helped shape modern marine aviation. Seattle: Self published

243. Sweller, J., van Merrienboer, J. J., Paas, F. G. (1998). Cognitive architecture and instructional design. *Educational Psychology Review*, 10(3), 251-296.

244. Tabachnick, B. G., & Fidell, L. S. (2007). *Using multivariate statistics* (5th ed.). Boston, MA: Allyn and Bacon.

245. Temple, E. C., & Brown, R. F. (2012). A comparison of internet-based participant recruitment methods: Engaging the hidden population of cannabis users in research. *Journal of Research Practice*, 7(2), 2.

246. Tinsley, E.A., and Brown, S.D. (2000). *Applied Multivariate Statistics and Mathematical Modeling.* Burlington, NJ: Elsevier.

247. Torres, R. H. (2008). Embracing a safety culture in coast guard aviation. In Stolzer, A. J., Halford, C.D., & Goglia, J. J. (Eds.) *Safety management systems in aviation.* (pp.161-267). Burlington, VT: Ashgate.

248. Vallée, G., Pernet, R., & Urdiroz, A. (2015, July). Fuel monitoring on the A320 family aircraft. *The Airbus Safety magazine, Safety First*, 22, 30-37.

249. Vallerand, R. J. (2008). On the psychology of passion: In search of what makes people's lives most worth living. *Canadian Psychology*, 49(1), 1-13.

250. Vallerand, R. J., Blanchard, C., Mageau, G. A., Koestner, R., Ratelle, C., Léonard, M., et al. (2003). Les passions de l'âme: On obsessive and harmonious passion. *Journal of Personality and Social Psychology*, 85, 756–767.

251. Vidulich, M. A., & Tsang, P. S. (2015). The confluence of situation awareness and mental workload for adaptable Human–Machine systems. *Journal of Cognitive Engineering and Decision Making*, 9(1), 95-97. doi:10.1177/1555343414554805

252. Vidulich, M., A., Wickens, C., D., Tsang, P., S., & Flack, J., M. (2010). Information processing in aviation. In Salas E. & Maurino, D. (Eds.), *Human factors in aviation* (2nd ed.) (pp. 175-215). Burlington, MA: Academic Press – Elsevier.

253. Vogt, W. P., Gardner, D., C., & Haeffele, L., M. (2012). *When to use what research design.* Guilford press. New York; New York.

254. Volz, E.; Wejnert, C.; Cameron, C.; Spiller, M.; Barash, V.; Degani, I.; and Heckathorn, D.D. (2012). Respondent-Driven Sampling Analysis Tool (RDSAT) Version 7.1. Ithaca, NY: Cornell University.

255. Wainer, H., & Kiely, G. L. (1987). Item clusters and computerized adaptive testing: A case for testlets. *Journal of Educational Measurement*, 24(3), 185-201.

256. Walcott, C. M., & Phillips, M. E. (2013). *The effectiveness of computer-based cognitive training programs.* Bethesda.

257. Warner, R. M. (2013). Applied Statistics: from bivariate through multivariate technique (3rd ed.), Thousand Oaks, CA: Sage Publications Ltd.

258. Wejnert, C., & Heckathorn, D.D. (2008). Web-based network sampling: efficiency and efficacy of respondent-driven sampling for online research *Sociological Methods and Research*.

259. Wensveen, J. G. (2011). *Air Transportation: A management perspective.* Burlington, VT: Ashgate Publishing.

260. Westland, C. J. (2010). Lower bounds on sample size in structural equation modeling. *Electronic Commerce Research and Applications*, 9(6), 476-487. doi:10.1016/j.elerap.2010.07.003

261. Weyer, J. (2016). Confidence in hybrid collaboration. an empirical investigation of pilots' attitudes towards advanced automated aircraft. *Safety Science*, 89, 167-179. doi:10.1016/j.ssci.2016.05.008

262. Wickens, C. D. (2002). Situation awareness and workload in aviation. *Current Directions in Psychological Science*, 11(4), 128-133. doi:10.1111/1467-8721.00184

263. Wickens, C. D., Gordon-Becker, S. E., Liu, Y., & Lee, J. D. (2004). *An introduction to human factors engineering* (2nd ed.). Upper Saddle River, NJ: Pearson Education.

264. Wickens, C. D., Sebok, A., Gore, B.F., & Hooey, B. L. (2012). Predicting pilot error in NextGen: pilot performance modeling and validation efforts. *Proceedings of the 4th International Conference on Applied Human Factors and Ergonomics* (AHFE), July 2012

265. Wiegmann, D. A., Zhang, H., von Thaden, T., Sharma, G., & Mitchell, A. (2002). *Safety culture: A review.* (Technical Report No. ARL-02-3/FAA-02-2). Atlantic City, NJ: FAA.

266. Williams, B. (2012). Exploratory factor analysis: A five step guide. *Journal of Emergency Primary Health Care* (JEPHC)(8)3.

267. Wise, M. A. (2011). *Pilot knowledge of automated flight controls: Implications for designing training based on adult learning principles* (Doctoral dissertation, Oklahoma State University).

268. Wise, A., Abbott, D. W., Wise, J. A., & Wise, S. A. (2010). Underpinnings of System Evaluation. In J. A. Wise, V. D. Hopkin, & D. J. Garland (Eds.), *Handbook of aviation human factors* (2nd ed.) (pp. 4-1-4-16). Boca Raton, FL: CRC Press – Taylor & Francis.

269. Woodley, X. M. (2014). *Black women's faculty voices in New Mexico: Invisible assets silent no more* (Order No. 3579922). Available from ProQuest Dissertations & Theses Global. (1517932102).

270. Woodley, X. M., & Lockard, M. (2016). Womanism and snowball sampling: Engaging marginalized populations in holistic research. *The Qualitative Report*, 21(2), 321-329.

271. Woo, G. S. (2015). Starting a safety management system culture in small flight school organizations. *Journal of aviation/aerospace education & research*, 24(3).

272. Yantiss, B. (2011). SMS Implementation. In Stolzer, A. J., Halford, C.D., & Goglia, J. J. (Eds.) *Safety management systems in aviation.* (pp. 161-267). Burlington, VT: Ashgate.

273. Young, J. P., Fanjoy, R. O., & Suckow, M. W. (2006). *Impact of glass cockpit experience on manual flight skills.* ERAU Scholarly Commons.

274. Yong, A. G., & Pearce, S. (2013) A Beginner's Guide to Factor Analysis: Focusing on Exploratory Factor Analysis, Tutorials in Quantitative Methods for Psychology, 9(2), 79-94. doi: 10.20982/

275. NTSB. (2019). Atlas Air Flight 3591 crashed into Trinity Bay. Report number: Accident number DCA 19MA086. Retrieved https://www.ntsb.gov/investigations/pages/dca19ma086.aspx

276. Federal Democratic Republic of Ethiopia Ministry of Transport Aircraft Accident Investigation Bureau (2019), Ethiopian Airlines Group. Report No. AI-01/19. Retrieved: https://leehamnews.com/wp-content/uploads/2019/04/Preliminary-Report-B737-800MAX-ET-AVJ.pdf

277. KNKT Republic of Indonesia (2018) Accident investigation report. Final KNKT. 18.10.35.04. Retrieved from http://knkt.dephub.go.id/knkt/ntsc_aviation/baru/2018%20-%20035%20-%20PK-LQP%20Final%20Report.pdf

Acknowledgements

THE RESEARCH BEHIND this book could not have come to fruition without consultation of a team of subject matter experts who gave freely not only of their time, but also shared their vast experience to assist in the future of aviation: Dr. Chris Broyhill, Captain Ray Wallace, Captain Tim Tobin, Captain Carl Davis, Captain Bo Corby, Captain John Doherty, Captain Jay Sakas, and First Officer Daniel Sallee. These professionals' experience (found in the body of this paper) and their willingness to give their valuable time is what made this project a success.

Many individuals also assisted along the way. My proctor Dr. Johnny Summers, an Alaska Airlines Captain, FAA designee, and aviation enthusiast, provide his masterful proctoring skills, but more than that—unending support.

Many representatives of organizations stepped forward to help share the survey information: Alitalia, Allied Pilots Association, Spanish Union of Airline Pilots (SELPA), Female Aviators Standing Together (FAST), ERAU, 99s, and Curt Lewis, as did many individuals. Armond Angeles, who was my go to stats guru, provided assistance that was invaluable.

My committee: Dr. Alan Stolzer introduced me to Safety Management Systems and the quintessential importance of safety culture in airline operations. Dr. Haydee Cuevas introduced me to adaptive expertise and shared her expertise in human factors, helped take my writing to the doctoral level, and her overall support and compassion were like none other. Dr. Tony Kern continually reminds me that professionalism and associated behavior will make the skies safer. He gave his valuable time to add operational realism as an aviator with expertise for safety and human reliability to improve this work. Dr. Dave Esser, the professor who had the most daunting task of the chair, showed patience and perseverance, and reminded me that good things take time. Dr. Cortes posed excellent operational questions that assisted in providing clarity. Dr. Friend stepped in as interim associate dean and added his editing expertise. Dr. Dothang Truong provided valuable help through this program with his statistical expertise and willingness to always answer questions, and was the driving force for my first published article. Daniel L. Hammes, ERAU Campus Director Seattle, San Francisco Bay, and Tacoma Campuses, represents the essence of aviation passion; and throughout this process he stood by my side supporting the future of aviation which reminded me why this research was important.

A huge thanks to Jennifer Hunt and Jen Edwards, my cohort sisters, for the laughter and challenges we shared daily along this journey. I would like to acknowledge all those in my cohort and those I shared classes with, and inspired critical thinking along the way, and for Troy for his continued support and our very enjoyable legal debates in Aviation Law.

My mother, Pat Kassner, gave her unending support in the pursuit of my education and supported me with all that has transpired as a result of this work. Lee Seham reduced the weight off my shoulders while finishing my dissertation, and inspired me as to the type of attorney I will become.

This book would not be complete without Nathan Everett at ElderRoadBooks@outlook.com, who brings great books to life, Tony Stieber who took his time for the initial edit, and Captain John Nance, Dr. Chris Broyhill, and Captain Eric Auxier for their support of aviation safety.

Last but not least, I thank my husband, Dick Petitt, who is a partner in this research and my life. He is the person I bounced ideas off of, read my work to, and who understood that the pursuit of this education was more than just a plaque on the wall. When the lessons of SMS and safety culture opened my eyes to operational reality, he stood by my side throughout the ensuing and unexpected path we traveled. His unending support and encouragement to do the right thing on behalf of safety have made the skies just a little bit safer. Three novels have sprung from this research and are definitely worth the read—*Flight for Sanity, Flight For Truth, and coming in 2021 Flight For Justice. Nobody should ever be retaliated against for reporting safety concerns.*

ABOUT THE AUTHOR

KARLENE PETITT IS an international airline pilot who is type-rated, and has flown and/or instructed on the B777, B747-400, B747-200, B767, B757, B737, B727, and A330 aircraft. She has been a pilot for 41 years, holds MBA and MHS degrees, and earned her PhD in Aviation, with a focus on safety, from Embry Riddle Aeronautical University. Petitt is a mother of three, grandmother of eight, and author who has written numerous books in multiple genres. Novels: *Flight For Control, Flight For Safety, Flight For Survival, Flight for Sanity, and Flight For Truth. Motivation: Flight to Success: Be the Captain of your Life.* For the children: *I am Awesome, the ABCs of being me.*

KARLENE IS AVAILABLE to host aviation discussion groups, join book clubs, or speak at your meetings.

Please email her at Karlene.Petitt@gmail.com to schedule your next event. And check out her blog for more writings at KarlenePetitt.com

www.ingramcontent.com/pod-product-compliance
Lightning Source LLC
LaVergne TN
LVHW011326080426
835513LV00006B/209